MW01232705

22

Without A Clue

From "Lost & Confused" to Getting Paid to Live Your Best Life

22 Without A Clue

From "Lost & Confused" to Getting Paid to Live Your Best Life

Ordering Information & Quantity Sales: Special discounts are available on quantity purchases by corporations, associations, and others. For details, contact the publisher. Orders by U.S. & International trade bookstores and wholesalers at: info@abundantpress.com. Printed in the United States of America- Library of Congress-in-Publication Data. Please note: This book was put together very quickly for a conference, so if you find errors, like spelling or grammar, please send us an email.

Title:22 Without A Clue
Sub-title: From "Lost & Confused" to Getting Paid to Live Your Best Life
Author: Sean D. Gray
1. The main category of the book — Business, Personal Development. Success
First Edition, First Printing June 1st, 2020
ISBN: 978-1-948287-17-3

To Get FREE Access Additional Bonuses Visit:
SeanDGray.com

Foreword

By Tom Hopkins

Over the course of my life, I've been blessed to meet literally hundreds of thousands of people. Most were attendees at the various seminars I have led around the world. It's been my life's work to teach and train those who have chosen the profession of selling as a career or to utilize selling skills in growing their business and personal relationships.

My goal in training has always been two-fold: First, to teach powerfully effective communication skills. Second, to inspire my students that there is greatness within them—that they are only limited by their own thoughts and actions. Many of my students benefited more from that second part of my mission than the first. They became more than students of selling. They became students of life. I have been humbled by the accomplishments they attribute to having their eyes opened through my teachings.

When I first met Sean Gray, I knew there was something different about him. I could tell he was not just taking in knowledge but demonstrated a burning desire to experience its impact. As the author Anthony Douglas Williams has said, "Knowledge comes from learning. Wisdom comes from living." Through the knowledge he gained, Sean began living his dream life, and has achieved a level of wisdom rarely found in someone so young. He has invested the time and effort necessary to become wise beyond his years.

I am thrilled that Sean has written this book, at this time, from his unique perspective. I have often wondered how my life would have been different if I hadn't learned so many lessons the hard way, and perhaps had learned them earlier in life. You, dear reader, have the opportunity within these pages to get a head start on living the life of your dreams.

The accumulated knowledge within these pages is powerful. It can shortcut your way to success—as *you* define it—but only when you apply it. Use it to unlock the barriers to success that you now see before you. Be ready to enter a wonderful cycle of growth and change at an accelerated pace by following Sean's advice.

Tom Hopkins
Speaker **&** Best-Selling Author
Author of:
- How to Master the Art of Selling
- Low Profile Selling
- When Buyers Say No
- The Gentle Art of Persuasion
- The Language of Sales
- Sell it Today, Sell it Now
- Selling in Tough Times
- Selling for Dummies
- The Official Guide to Success
- 16 Power Closes & More

ENDORSEMENTS

From Mentors

"Be ready to enter a wonderful cycle of growth and change at an accelerated pace by following Sean's advice."

Tom Hopkins
Best-Selling Author, How to Master the Art of Selling

"What do you do when it doesn't pay off to be exceptional? When college students enter a new playing field with old rules? Sean's experiences, insights, and strategy empower a whole new wave of talent. I can't wait to see this in more hands."

Katriel C Sarfati
Founder GrowthHaxx

From Students

"Sean's lessons and strategies have opened my eyes to the full potential of what my life can be, without his words and inspiration I'd be stuck living the life someone else set out for me and not going after the life I want to live"

Shawn Winters
Remote Work Expert (Age 30)

"Very helpful. I strongly recommend that most people get into this and break out of the typical ways we look at money."

Irubiel Moreno
Artist (Age 26)

"Sean's seven step process to lifestyle freedom opened my mind to how I could actually attain it. Since learning this, my vision has become a reality and I'm getting paid to live instead of living to get paid."

Bryan Fobbs
Founder, Be Fobbs Fit (Age 25)

ACKNOWLEDGEMENTS

- **To My Dad:** *Thank you for challenging me to ask better questions, being my greatest mentor and showing me how the 'real world' really works.*

- **To My Mentors:** *Thank you for encouraging me to keep going, for the generosity of sharing your time with me and the many life and business lessons you've helped me master.*

- **To Andy Broadway:** *Thank you for your patience and brilliant efforts in turning this book into a reality for me.*

- **To You, The Reader:** *Thank you for investing in yourself and having the desire to grow. You're the one who's capable of changing the world and I'm honored to be a part of your journey.*

DEDICATION

This book is dedicated to my mom. Thank you for your unconditional love and support as I attempted to figure out life.

I will continue to remember who I am and be a blessing. We'll be together soon. I love you.

Cheri Gray
Feb. 12, 1960 - Dec. 13, 2019

Contents

PROLOGUE

"There are two ways to conquer and enslave a nation.
One is by the sword. The other is by debt."
–John Adams

Your training wheels are coming off. You're going from your well-known structure of society as it was laid out for you by your parents, the school system and just about every institution or organization you've been a part of until now.

You're being thrown into the 'real world' with little to no 'real world' experience – and you're about to be if you haven't been already – faced with major life decisions that ONLY you are responsible for.

That means no more mom and dad to fall back on, no more teachers making sure you do your work, no more coaches making sure you show up to practice or eat right, no more step by step curriculum to get you through *"graduation"*, and no more make up tests... In fact, in the 'real world' you get the test first, then the lesson. Every method of operation you're accustomed to is changing.

The feeling you might be experiencing is complete confusion. It's as if you were just launched into space and now, you're floating with no direction. You might be looking for something familiar to latch onto; another structure to fit in.

But before you do that and before you make major commitments about your future, I encourage you to go through a transformative process that will not only give you clarity on the exact lifestyle you want to live and what truly fulfills you, but also dramatically accelerate your success.

Some of you might be thinking, *"Not me, Sean. I know exactly what I'm going to do now that I'm in the real world."* If this is you and you have a plan, you're excited about executing, then awesome! Go for it with passion. Nonetheless, I ask you to entertain the idea that you – just as I was – might be unaware of some real-world truths that may have the power to incredibly enhance your current vision of your future.

I didn't write this book because I've achieved some higher wisdom, I feel qualified to preach or because I've made hundreds of millions of dollars. Rather, this book was written because I was fortunate enough to be guided by incredible mentors through a rare process, I'm about to share with you. If there is anything that helps you here, it will be because of them and not me.

I'm simply organizing it into a book because I know this information helped me as I made one of the biggest transitions in life.

This book is about freedom.

"But, Sean, I want money and a lot of it. I want the 'good life'."

I understand. I think it's safe to say that most people want the 'good life'.

That was my approach when I first got out of college too. I thought money was the answer to the struggle. I was in for a rude awakening when I got the good life and discovered I wasn't fulfilled. Even in spite of enjoying how I was making the money, something was missing.

This will make more sense when you experience it.

Jim Carrey said, *"I wish everyone could get rich and famous and have everything they ever dreamed of so they will know that it's not the answer."*

I believe there are no shortcuts in life. You have to go through the processes. And while you can't circumvent the process, you can speed it up. That is what I hope this book does for you. So instead of me telling you that financial freedom will not necessarily give you a happy life, I am going to help you move along the journey faster so you can achieve what you want, but hopefully and more importantly step into personal freedom.

Albert Einstein once wisely stated, *"All religions, arts and sciences are branches of the same tree. All these aspirations are directed toward ennobling man's life, lifting it from the sphere of mere physical existence and leading the individual towards freedom."*

Now when I say this book is about freedom, what does the word freedom mean?

First, I believe there are different levels of freedom. There's Social freedom. Financial freedom. Personal freedom.

Thankfully most of us have social freedom – the ability to get a job, choose where we want to live, what food we buy, how we spend our time. We are not slaves in the common sense of the word.

What most of us seek within the monetary economic system is financial freedom. Unfortunately, that's where many people stop. And that's also generally the order it is approached, thinking that if we just get financial freedom, we will be happy and truly in control of our lives.

Nonetheless, it is nearly pointless to worry about financial freedom if you have no social freedom. And I can say from experience, it is very difficult, considering the society we've been raised in, to truly seek personal freedom before financial freedom. No matter how many people would have told me money wouldn't make me happy, I still had the urge to 'touch the stove for myself' so to speak and focus only on business and getting money. Then I started getting the money, more than I had imagined for myself at a young age, but I still found myself unfulfilled.

So, I implore you to remember in your core that money will NOT make you free in your heart, mind and soul. For if you forget this, the ego will win, you will have money – but you will also be a slave to it.

Don't worry, this book is not just a bunch of philosophical concepts. The practicality will come. I would be doing you a disservice if I didn't tell you the stove was hot before empowering you to touch it and learn from your experience.

With all that being said, I understand experience is the best teacher and you're probably still thinking, *"Okay, I get it but I still want and need money."* And I can completely relate.

In fact, I had one of the biggest arguments with my first real world mentor, who also happens to be my dad, around this exact thing. He was ultimately right, and through some careful explanation my eyes were opened to the bigger picture. My hope is that this book does the same for you.

I understand now that it is a fractal process to truly internalize values and concepts that contradict nearly everything you've learned and been taught your entire life. Again, it is a process. A transformation. There are steps, and steps inside those steps. Lessons and lessons within those lessons – some that make sense, and some that you don't quite understand yet. If you trust the process, it will all connect, and like Steve Jobs said, "You cannot connect the dots looking forward; you can only connect the dots looking backwards. So, you have to trust that the dots will somehow connect in your future."

In an effort to not circumvent the process but instead to help you speed it up, I've documented my transformation. I've taken thousands of pages of notes, captured the lessons my mentors taught me and lessons learned in failure, and boiled them down to a practical process.

Now I firmly believe you can't teach entrepreneurship or happiness or even freedom.

However, I do believe you can be guided into the best opportunities to grow and eventually live it for yourself.

Consider the rest of this book exactly that – foundational principles for you to start living right now; a guide to helping you master the real world and accelerate your success.

INTRODUCTION

Start Retired: Don't Live to Get Paid, Get Paid to Live

---

*"How in the hell could a man enjoy being awakened at 6:30
a.m. by an alarm clock, leap out of bed, dress, force-feed, shit,
piss, brush teeth and hair, and fight traffic to get to a place
where essentially you made lots of money for somebody else
and were asked to be grateful for the opportunity to do so?"*
— **Charles Bukowski**

Remember when you were young, and told that if you go to school and get good grades, then you will be able to get a great job? Your life will be easy; you will work till you're 60 and then retire and live your golden years doing all the things that you've always dreamed of. Sound familiar?

We've all been told the same thing in one form or another. What's more, most of us have gone down that exact path that was outlined to us. Many have probably been quite successful doing it.

Perhaps you graduated with honors or were successful in getting into the college of your dreams.

Or maybe you landed a great job. That's great. You deserve it because I'm sure you put all your effort into the pursuit of that great job.

But here's something you should consider: have you taken the time to look around at the real world today? Have you ever looked at the people around you who are very successful and quite wealthy? Do you believe they achieved their success because of what they learned in school?

Or do you think they achieved their current lifestyle from their job? Have you ever wondered why some people accomplish great success at such an early stage in their life? Have you ever thought about how these people accomplished all that they have today?

It makes perfect sense, doesn't it, that if you want to be rich and successful, you would want to know how other rich and successful people accomplished it. Keep in mind that I'm not referring to celebrities or tech geniuses. I'm talking about normal people – just like you and me – who found the secret path to wealth and success. I can safely say that they didn't achieve this success by getting good grades or by going to the college of their dreams. They certainly didn't get rich and wealthy by working for somebody else.

Don't get me wrong. I'm not saying that you shouldn't go to college. Or that you shouldn't have a job. I went to college. It was one of the greatest experiences of my life. I built some lifelong relationships. What I am saying is that simply going to school and landing a job is not going to make you rich and successful.

The only way you will be content with working for someone else is if your dream life includes being told where to be, when to be there, what to do, how to do it etc. I would recommend that if you do take a job, you should do it for experience rather than money.

Most of us fall into the same pattern. We go to school. We get good grades. We get into the right college. We find the right job. Our story is the same as many other millennials. But the time will come when you will ask yourself, what do I do to make money now?

It seems like a valid question, but I'm sorry to break the news to you that it's the wrong question altogether.

My dad always told me: *"If you want great answers, you have to ask great questions."*

Your mind is very powerful and it can solve any problem you give it. Many of my peers and others before me got out of school and followed the same path. They were making money but only enough to pay their bills and hit the bars after work. Sound familiar?

Some of us realized pretty quickly that something wasn't right. They might have a job but they had no control over their life. They had no freedom.

You will soon realize that the real world is nothing like your life in school. Nobody taught you anything about banking in school. Nobody taught you how to build your credit, apply for a loan or do your taxes. Nobody taught you how to set up entities or read a financial statement.

You did learn about the Pythagorean Theorem but did it help you in the real world? I doubt it.

The fact is that you are all on your own in the real world with absolutely no real-world practice and very little real-world knowledge. And so, you ask yourself the entrapping question: *What can I do to make money?*

How do you make money? Are you a server? Store manager? Work in Corporate America?

Maybe you should run your own local business? Or maybe you're searching for a job.

Whatever it might be, the question is: *Do you enjoy doing what it requires?* Do you think you can continue to do it till you retire? Can you see yourself doing it every day? If the answer to these questions is no, don't fret. You're not alone. The good news is that there are many ways to produce income – ways that are more fulfilling and freer.

I will share with you three steps that you should implement in your everyday life. If you do, the opportunity to make all the money you could ever possibly need will present itself, but more importantly, you'll be able to live your dream life sooner than you think.

Trust me, this is not some "get rich quick scheme" nor is this a sales pitch for a product that claims to put $100K in your bank account by the end of the month. What this will be, however, is the foundation of a transformational process.

WHY DO YOU NEED MONEY?

The first thing you need to understand is that your end goal is not money. Your end goal is achieving the lifestyle you want.

Your goal should be to build something that is long-lasting. You want money, not for the sake of having it but for the sake of using it to get the lifestyle you want.

Therefore, while you aspire to make money, you need to understand that the goal of making this money is not the money itself but what you can do with it.

Most people get side tracked because of the money dilemma. They fall into this trap because they think they need to earn money to afford the good life or raise their family or send their children to a renowned college.

I don't blame you if you are in this trap as well.

We are raised most of our lives thinking that this is what we should be doing. This trap that I'm talking about is a way of thinking that was imposed on you your entire life. It was reinforced by teachers, the media, even politicians. Even your parents are to blame. You were taught that if you stayed in school, got good grades, attended a good college, found a good job and saved money, you'd be able to retire by the time you're 60 (if you work really, really hard, maybe by the time you're 40!)

We go along with this narrative because we don't know any better. We are never given the opportunity to think outside this domain. We might have this inner voice telling us to do something different, but that voice is always shut down by expectations.

We are expected to behave in a certain manner and if we don't conform, we fail. Or so we think. This pressure to conform makes us fall deeper and deeper into the money trap. We spend our lives running around for that paycheck. We have no time to follow our dreams; no time to think big. And so, it goes on and on. Each day we follow the same routine and the same pattern.

Does this sound familiar? Are you in this same situation? If you are, you better think about it now.

That's because the next thing you'll know is it's 15 years later, and you're still at the same spot where you began.

It's time to get out of this trap. Don't live to get paid. Get paid to live. Design the lifestyle you want to live and then build streams of income that support that lifestyle. Freedom and transformation. That's what this book is.

CHANGE THE WAY YOU THINK

It's time to change your paradigm. Money has nothing to do with what you have in the bank – it has everything to do with your lifestyle. Instead of focusing on the money, you have to live a life that's guided by your desires rather than your fears. Holding that money in the bank is creating a "safety deposit" for you, a deposit that provides some insurance against anxiety and uncertainty.

You must realize that money is not stacks of bills. Money doesn't have to be a security blanket. You don't want to earn money just to know that it's there. You need money to give you the lifestyle you want.

"People say time is money, but that's not true at all. You can always make more money. You can never make more time. Time is more than money. Time is everything."

People lying on their deathbeds rarely say "I wish I had more money." Do they even say it at all? They almost always wish that they had more time.

They never found the "why" they needed to help them break free from the trap that is money.

Even worse, today we see the tides have turned against retirement. What I see increasingly is older individuals running out of money even before they run out of time.

To find happiness, you must live your life in a way that doesn't make you wish for more time at your deathbed. You have to live every day, taking full advantage of it and the time that you have available. Not saving up enough money to hopefully one day do all the things you've really wanted to do your whole life.

Making that happen is about building streams of income around the lifestyle you want to live instead of trading your precious time for money. In the grand scheme of things, trading your time for money is pointless. It's the exact opposite of freedom – it's *servitude*.

Changing the way, you think starts from this first realization, this first revelation. You must let go of the way you have interacted with money for most of your life. So many people are trapped in the cycle of money because they don't realize they don't have to be trapped OR how to escape the vicious cycle.

Who you are and how you understand money has been formulated over the course of years? Reversing that won't happen in just a few minutes or a few hours. The journey you're about to embark upon will get uncomfortable at times. You'll have to push yourself and find some discipline that will carry you along the way. I'm here to walk you down the path to finding that discipline, to creating structures that will make it all work for you.

As young people, we're not as afraid of change as the generations that came before us. Our views on financial security and wealth were formulated during a time of economic upheaval.

The rules and the routines our predecessors and we considered solid were erased in the span of just a few years. Those years fundamentally changed our outlook.

We had to learn to think outside the box to survive. As a result, we're malleable enough to change our paradigms. For an early twenties' person, life is a winding path that's full of twists and turns rather than a straight line from here to there.

Can you speed up that financial path? The answer is unequivocal *yes*. This book was created to help you collapse time frames and accelerate your growth.

IT'S TIME TO REDEFINE RETIREMENT

I believe it's time to redefine retirement. This is another age-old concept that's been ingrained in our brains. The idea is that we can only retire when we're old and grey. Why? Says who? Do we have to wait for a tragedy to start changing our life? Do we have to wait for something serious to happen to decide this is it, I'm done?

What if I told you that by the time, I was 24, in the traditional sense of the word, I was retired?

You might be thinking I'm full of shit or you might be wondering how I did it.

Let me explain why you can start out in the real world already retired.

Think about the definition. What is retirement? Retirement is when you can do what you want to do when you want to do it. The myth that retirement is about living on a fixed income and battling the challenges of age is just that: a myth.

To put it in simple terms, retirement is the period of life when you're done working for money. Age does not define when retirement's going to happen.

I can decide what to do with my time. It's *my* time now. I'm not bound to my bank account, a boss, an office, a system. The whole point of having the money is to have the freedom to choose the things that you do or don't want to do with your time. I can head down to the local coffee shop, and people watch for half a day. I can sit home in my pajamas and eat Cheerios while I binge on my favorite Netflix show all morning.

The moment you're no longer living to get paid but start getting paid to live life on your terms is the moment you're retired. If you're still struggling to see how you can get paid to live, the seven steps in this book with take you on a transformative journey to living that way. But it's a process, so don't wait.

The trouble is you think you have time. It's extremely dangerous to think you have time.

Time is precious, and the time is now. Time isn't tomorrow or yesterday; you're living time at this moment. Procrastination is a problem that hounds us all, especially when we're young. I'm guilty of it. It's a dangerous game to put off until tomorrow things that we should be doing to create our lives. Figuring out how to stop waiting while at the same time being patient in lessons is a central theme of this book.

Not realizing that your time is limited is a risky game. You probably think you have months, even years to accomplish your goals, so you may keep putting off retirement until there's no time left or until the time that you do have is limited by the realities of age. Even worse, something unexpected could come out of the blue to derail your retirement plan.

That last reality is what my mom lived through. She had just found a new passion to pursue, only to be hit with the news that she had cancer. Before her diagnosis, she thought she had time. With the cancer diagnosis, life handed her something that suddenly sucked up all her time, her attention, her energy. She was no longer able to decide what she wanted to do; she was faced with this life or death battle that could not be ignored.

But did she give up? No. This was not the time to give up.

You don't need to wait for a tragedy to change the course of your life.

My mom ultimately ended up losing the fight to cancer. But her battle put things in perspective. There is no guarantee of time to do the things you want to do.

There's no guarantee that your retirement will be waiting for you at the end of your working years.

Don't wait for a life-changing event to come and push you into change. Make the decision now to change your life from the inside. Transform the way you think about retirement, money and time will change your life for the better. Let me tell you a bit more about my transformative journey.

FOR THIS BOOK TO WORK, YOU HAVE TO FIND YOUR WHY

For young people, that *why* gets wrapped up in the conversation about time. We always feel like time is out there, that we've got plenty of it just to chill and drift through seasons of our life. It's only later in life that most people realize there is a literal deadline that seems to be approaching faster and faster as life goes on.

If you can realize that you've got to find your *why* right now, you stand a chance of making everything work out in a way that's fulfilling and meaningful. There's fulfillment in doing things out of purpose rather than to make a few bucks.

Nearly everyone has an experience in their life when they discover their major purpose; their definite reason for it all.

That moment for me was finding out about my mother's cancer. I was in a bad place. I had hit an all-time low. I had no mojo.

In an attempt to snap out of it, I went to an event. It was majorly recharging – I felt alive and wonderful about where things were going.

When I got home, I was on one of those amazing ups, recharged and ready to take the world on. I felt like I could do anything in life.

Then I got the call from Mom. She had been diagnosed with stage IV non-Hodgkin's lymphoma. When you hear cancer, you think death; you think it's over. It was, without a doubt, the worst news I'd ever gotten. I lost all motivation to pursue my goals. There was no reason, no purpose in trying to make things happen anymore. Life was nothing but fear and darkness.

My mom is the rock of our family. She's our foundation. I projected out into the future as though I had already lost her. Her diagnosis left me feeling there was no reason to go forward because she wasn't going to be there with me.

And if we all die, well what's the point of working on anything? That was my thinking.

I learned of Mom's diagnosis and I did nothing. I slept for 12 or more hours a day. Making my mom proud was everything to me. It's all I wanted out of life. I felt like a failure, wholly unworthy of her warmth.

My emotions and my outlook spiraled into an abyss that sucked me deeper and deeper into unhappiness.

The worst part of cancer is the uncertainty. You never know what's in your future. When you come to think about it, life isn't that much different, even in the absence of serious illness. There is no certainty that tomorrow is coming for any of us.

Still, we don't question the coming of the next day. Cancer makes you realize that tomorrow might not be coming. Such a powerful realization is obviously terrifying.

Sitting at my desk, I glanced up to see a card from my *'Why'*. It was one of those striking moments in life, a mirror image of the moment that the phone call had come to destroy my world. At that moment, I found clarity and purpose. I decided to turn *living how I want* into my profession and to live with a sense of urgency.

I wanted to spend as much time as I could with my mom. I wanted to provide the funds that could help her get the best treatment possible. I also needed to live in the real world, pay the bills and eat. Life costs money even when it's the worst or best of times. How was I going to afford all of this?

Asking myself these questions, I saw it all laid out before me. I needed to get paid to live. I needed freedom. I could face the fear and the doubt that came with cancer, free from the cage of financial insecurity. I didn't have to fight these battles on both fronts at the same time.

Don't wait for a life-changing experience to make the decision to change your life for the better.

A major *why* for me is to help young people collapse timeframes and move more quickly towards a life of freedom and fulfillment. I feel deeply fulfilled when I witness people who are empowered to live the lifestyle that they want right now – remember, no more waiting!

I am compelled to help others find their *why* before life pushes them as my mom's cancer pushed me.

Facing a personal tragedy isn't the only path to get motivation, though it is a path that so many people find themselves walking. My goal is to expose my peers to concepts and strategies that will offer them that same transformation in a self-directed way that's not dependent on heartache for growth.

Regardless of where you're at; whether you're in high school, college, grad school, the workforce, in a transition, etc., you can benefit from working on you. Your mind is a constant battlefield, always fine-tuning and working on skills, setting goals and taking actions. Learning to channel your power through your *why* is central to how you'll be able to create the life that you want.

Through this book, you will learn what it takes to uncover your personal *why*. This is a process of self-discovery. Don't be afraid to step up and explore your possibilities.

FINDING YOUR UNIQUE PURPOSE

I honestly believe we know our purpose in life at an early age. We may not be able to articulate it but we know it in our heart. We are born into greatness but conditioned into mediocrity. We can break free from the system; it just takes asking the right questions.

Here's one such question:
What value do you truly want to add to the world?

Your existence will have an impact on the world in some way. It's your choice whether you want your impact to be helpful or harmful. I can promise you that if your motive for doing anything is solely based on money, you will either fail or be unfulfilled when you succeed.

You need something more to drive you – a deeper purpose to get you through the challenges that are ahead. Look for what's beyond you. Then use that as a fuel for the fire inside. Decide to manifest your *why* into something real, rather than just letting it remain a concept.

When you begin to build a stream of income around your *why*, around the value you want to bring the world, that's the moment you will feel retired. That's the moment you'll be free.

A job is a single-point failure. You have one client - your boss. What will happen if you lose that job?

This new path will take time and it will take trust but it will pay off. I know how hard it is to invest money into intangibles when you don't have it, but this book will outline how to make it happen. I'll share the strategies that have helped me manifest my reality, the life that I want. It is possible and everyone has a starting point. Your starting point could be in a wide variety of places. What matters is that you recognize you'll never get there if you don't begin.

The butterfly effect is real. Once you commit to change, you'll see the effect in action. One relationship leads to another, then another, then another, all the way to me writing this book.

Life blossoms out of one decision to move forward, one step on the path of your life's destiny.

This book will help you discover your Major Definite Purpose (MDP).

You'll learn how to overcome your limiting beliefs, find out which questions to ask, and be exposed to the way the real world works to navigate, fulfill and build your MDP. Then you'll learn how to turn all of that into income and freedom.

You'll be introduced to the mandatory skills you'll need to build the financial machine to make it all happen. You'll set up a foundation so you'll have the tools to incorporate the change in your everyday reality. You'll also learn strategies to master immediate retirement.

Entrepreneurs invest money to make the machine that will solve more people's problems. This is a major part of the paradigm shift that's needed for you to find success beyond the normal paths laid out for you. You're no longer working for money – you're working for a lifestyle. Making that shift is critical. This book will help you find the answers.

There is no such thing as overnight success. Even those seemingly instant winners of *The Voice, X-Factor*, or *American Idol* took years to train and practice before they made it to that final stage. This book will equip you with the tools, strategies, and knowledge you need to become empowered and make it to where you want to be.

Don't give up on your dreams. You don't need to be stuck in the money trap. Now is the moment to make it happen. Not tomorrow, not next week, not when you're done with school nor after your first child is born. If you've ever asked yourself when you should dig in and take that next step, the answer is right now. ***Turn the page and let's get started.***

CHAPTER 1.
STEP 1 – CHANGE THE WAY YOU THINK

"How you think about a problem is more important than the problem itself. So always think positively."
- Norman Vincent Peale

Graduating from college is an important milestone. It's a massive transition that takes us from being under the shelter of our family to achieving independence on our own. It's a transition from the shelter of a closed environment to the Real World.

When I graduated from college, my family was going through a difficult time. People weren't getting along, and there was a lot of confusion. Have you had one of these moments when it seems like the timing is completely off, and all the important things in your life seem to be falling apart? It was one of those moments for me.

While this general state of confusion was happening, my dad reached out to me. He told me not to trap myself in mundane situations or make long-term commitments with no context. He offered to show me different opportunities that were available for me; opportunities I'd never considered.

This interaction changed my relationship with him.

I became intensely aware of the influence and success that my father had. What's more important, I got some perspective on how he got there.

Taking ownership of our successes is an important part of our psychological development. Taking pride in our achievements is critical to finding happiness. For a long time, however, I felt my success in life was mostly due to my father. I felt as though I had to hide his influence or else people would think that he was the sole reason for my success, rather than my own efforts. I was afraid they would say I only got where I was because of my father. So, I kept his help a secret.

It was at this point that I had another touchstone conversation with my dad. Once again, he gave me the guidance I needed to overcome my negative mindset. He told me that he wasn't the key to my success, that all he did was present the opportunities. He did the same for all the people in his life, from friends to business acquaintances.

Learning to take control of the way you think is transformative. The better you're able to master your thoughts, the better you'll be able to master your life.

For me, letting go of the feeling that I lived in the shadow of my father's success allowed me to expand my own. It started with not caring about what other people think, a function of letting go of my ego. And believe me – ego is powerful enough to make you turn down possibilities.

It's possible to transform your thinking, and this will lead to a transformation of your life. What you think and believe affects how you behave.

How you behave affects the results you produce. If you want to change the results you're producing in life, first change the way you think.

YOUR MIND IS YOUR STRONGEST ASSET

A mind IS a terrible thing to waste.

Your mind is more powerful than any other tool you have at your disposal: money, connections, resources or anything else. It is your mind that attracts the money, connections and opportunities. The power of your mind moves your body into action, inspires you to take hold of opportunities, brings you the clarity to focus on the task at hand. And that leads you toward the future. Life is an amalgamation of experiences that exist in our minds and is colored by our perceptions.

Mastering your thoughts is the key to controlling your mind and moving toward success. You will soon realize that success is not something that you attain; it is something that you strive towards.

Success is progress. Any progress you make in the right direction can be defined as success. In other words, success is a constant act and a continuous choice that you make each day. You'll find that your life can only move forward if you are in control of your mind. That's an easy thing to say, but it's an incredibly challenging thing to do. That's one of the ways this book will help you.

Learning to leverage the mind's power is simpler than you probably realize but getting there requires a methodical approach and commitment to the process.

A thorough approach that you internalize will soon help you break the chains that hold your mind back.

One of the strongest features of our mind is that we have the power to change it. We have the power to change the way we think. And we can do so by surrounding ourselves with people who have a successful mindset.

Think of it this way: How do we learn to speak? Children don't learn to speak by studying words or learning the vowels or mastering punctuation. They learn to speak by being around people who speak to them. They acquire the skill by observing and learning from people who surround them. If you want to develop a successful mindset and if you want to learn how to grow and how to succeed, you need to hang around people who have that kind of mindset.

People often have more of a "glass half empty" outlook than they realize. This kind of negativity sneaks into life in small ways. You can relate to this with a simple example.

Let's say you've worked very hard to lose weight. You reach a point where you're not at your ideal body weight, but you're happy that you got to that point at least. You tend to relax. Slowly, your old eating habits start to sneak in. It starts with a donut. Or a chocolate bar. Or both. Slowly and gradually, your weight starts to increase.

You may not notice a difference initially, but in six months or a year, you will realize that you're overweight again. Unwanted habits can seep in and can have a significant impact on your life.

Negativity works the same way. You may be thinking about opportunities that seem out of reach, worrying about whether some cash flow will manifest. It can even be tied into smaller, every day, mundane occurrences. We have to decide whether to view life through optimistic or pessimistic glasses every minute.

These decisions focus on big things like relationships and small things like the internal thought process when we're alone.

Optimism is healthy. Study after study has shown that being an optimist leads to a longer life and better health. It's good for mental health, because pessimists can easily and quickly succumb to depression and anxiety from their negative mindsets. Pessimism is a habit, one that hangs around for far too long. Just like any habit, it's something that we can control if we choose to. It's not an easy path to walk, particularly if you've been a pessimist for a while.

A friend of mine, Kyle, lived through the worst year of his young adult life when we were in college. He was a junior with just over one year to go before he graduated. He found himself facing many challenges that stemmed from his actions (broken relationships, drunk driving and others). He also faced external challenges like serious family problems.

I learned a lot from Kyle during that time of his life. I learned about looking on the bright side and staying focused on the positive things. I learned to worry ONLY about the things I can control. A core lesson that Kyle taught me was that life has peaks and valleys, but everything passes. Circumstances are temporary, and if we persevere, we can surmount the challenges that come our way.

Understanding these lessons makes the times when you feel down seem manageable because you know it's temporary. You'll eventually rise again.

Every great person in history has been through hard times. The difference between the people who are remembered in the history books and those who are forgotten is that great minds have kept on going even in situations that appeared to be hopeless.

"It's hard to beat someone who never quits"- **Babe Ruth**

Stop thinking that others have goods handed to them on a silver platter. No one gets to success without a struggle. Even with every opportunity that can come your way, you will need optimism to see the chance and courage to use it. Opportunity is useless unless you take advantage of it; in the same way, knowledge only becomes power when it's applied.

Part of mastering your thoughts involves learning to look on the bright side of life as well as figuring out the right path to take. The steps you'll find outlined in this chapter will not only help you believe you can achieve whatever you set out to do, but also the steps will help you determine how to achieve it. Letting go of pessimism, adopting a positive attitude and outlining a game plan are some critical elements of success. Once you can learn to stay positive, you will be able to change your life.

Here's a quote I believe you will find pertinent to this topic:

"Our deepest fear is not that we are inadequate. Our deepest fear is that we are powerful beyond measure. It is our light, not our darkness that most frightens us."

We ask ourselves, Who am I to be brilliant, gorgeous, talented, fabulous?

Actually, who are you not to be? You are a child of God. You're playing small does not serve the world. There is nothing enlightened about shrinking so that other people won't feel insecure around you.

"...We are all meant to shine, as children do. We were born to make manifest the glory of God that is within us. It's not just in some of us; it's in everyone. And as we let our own light shine, we unconsciously give other people permission to do the same. As we are liberated from our own fear, our presence automatically liberates others." - **Marianne Williamson**

SURROUND YOURSELF WITH PEOPLE WHO HAVE A GROWTH MINDSET

The first real step in mastering your thoughts is to surround yourself with people who think with a successful, growth mindset. People in our lives have so much influence over us. If we surround ourselves with people who have a growth mindset, we are likely to follow the same path.

The way in which you communicate will depend on your lifestyle. For young people today, social media provide opportunities for interactions with positive people. Those are real relationships that have real influence in our lives.

One option is to take a break from social media when we feel that it has a negative influence. That's a great option, one that I fully endorse.

The other option is to fill social media with positive things, with messages and people who inspire and encourage one another. Social media shows you content based on the content you engage with. Stop liking pictures of celebrities, pointless memes and any content that doesn't help you grow. Instead, engage with personal development pages, business growth pages, positive, encouraging and uplifting content.

In the real world, it's not just about what you know, but who you know - who knows you - and more importantly HOW they know you. You have a unique story to tell and unique things to offer others. People will resonate with your message if you allow them to do so. Such compatibility can come from people you've just gotten to know.

Often, it's those encounters that are the most fulfilling. Following the same logic, brand-new acquaintances can also be the ones who have the most profoundly negative impact. Don't hold onto them!

You don't owe anyone anything, especially if their influence isn't serving you. One of the hardest lessons in life is learning to let go of your attachment to people who are not helping you grow. We can become addicted to the suffering or the complaining. It's ironic, but when we continually talk negatively, habits get formed in that regard.

Our habits become comfort zones for us, and thus we become habitually comfortable with negativity. This is a slippery slope. The angst those relationships bring into your life doesn't have to stay there. All you have to do is choose to let go. It doesn't have to be nasty, and there's no reason to bring more drama or impunity into the mix. Just let them go.

Even if it's only within yourself, make that break for your mental wellbeing.

Trust yourself. Trust your journey. Trust the timing and the process.

If you have a clear vision of what you need in your life, your time will come. Let go of the expectation that you have to compete with anyone. Your path is unique, and you're at a different point in the journey than others are in theirs.

While you might feel as though you are standing in someone's shadow, there is someone else standing in your shadow. For me, that perception stemmed from the relationship with my dad. Once I realized I didn't need to apologize for those opportunities, I was able to embrace the positive things he brought into my life. I could let go of shame; there is nothing enlightening about shrinking. I learned I had plenty to offer, regardless of the fact that my dad had so much to offer me.

Surround yourself with people that add value to your life and you'll find personal mastery a whole lot easier. There is no such thing as a self-made person; we are all a product of our relationships.

LIMITING BELIEFS

"It is our interpretation of the past, our limiting beliefs, and our undigested pain that stop us from being able to move forward with clear direction."
–Debbie Ford in "Find a New One"

Limiting beliefs are those thoughts that we hold very dear, but that are holding us back. We all have limiting beliefs.

Most often, these thoughts have been with us for a while. Just like our pessimism, limiting beliefs can be habit-forming. We believe we have to go work every day. We believe we haven't gotten enough education to make good money. We believe we'll never be free from debt or obligation. We often believe we'll never get the freedom to be the person we know we can be.

What Are Your Limiting Beliefs?

Take a moment to think about your limiting beliefs. The best way to do this is to go through each part of your life: career, finances, relationships, etc. What are your limits in those areas? Where does your autonomy stop? What can't you do?

Those are your limiting beliefs, those *I can't* statements. You've spent the time to get used to them. You like them. Now you're going to learn to let them go. Look back to your *why* from the introduction. This is where you start to engage the heart and the mind, expanding your path.

Comparing ourselves to others is one of the most common limiting beliefs. It holds people back more than anything else. It's self-sabotaging and it's keeping you from what you want in life. Social media contributes to self-sabotage via comparison in a big way.

Always look at social media and realize that what people put out there is rarely the real thing. It's a window, but it's not the whole picture. It's a highlight reel. It's where people present an illusion of their best selves for the world to see.

You can harness the power of relationships to demolish your limiting beliefs. Instead of comparing, try finding inspiration. Look at what other people are doing and follow their lead. Realize that those folks who seem to have it all together weren't always that way and very few people are real enough or vulnerable enough to post their struggles.

Limiting beliefs can also stem from how you approach your life. Do you operate with scarcity mentality or an abundance mentality? Are you a follower of a fixed-mentality approach or a growth-mentality approach?

The most important thing to understand is that people can achieve almost anything they want in their life by helping others get what they want. By doing so, it can become very easy to morph from living your life in scarcity to living your life in abundance. I strongly believe that by doing three things, you can transition from a scarcity mentality to an abundance mentality.

These three things include:
- Change the way you think.
- Get a mentor.
- Change the people you're around.

"Life is a tragedy when seen in close-up, but a comedy in long-shot. To truly laugh, you must be able to take your pain, and play with it!"
–Charlie Chaplin

Limiting beliefs are closely tied to our inability to see the big picture. For example, you might see a guy online really succeeding, which might leave you feeling inadequate. You'll get anxious, and start doubting yourself. You will never see the problems behind the scene – the strain on his relationship with his partner, loads of debt that he's carrying. You only see a small snapshot.

Looking at a problem through the wide-angle lens of time and space can make it seem much less significant and far less limiting.

SUCCESSFUL MIND
VS. UNSUCCESSFUL MIND

To create a successful mind, you have to give it the chance to be successful. Right now, you might unconsciously be doing things in life that are holding your mind back. Let's change that.

What are you doing with your spare time? There's no such thing as *spare time* in the world of successful people. Every moment is an opportunity to make something happen.

How do you spend your "spare" time? When you're waiting for a flight, or waiting in line, or waiting in traffic, are you on Facebook seeing what other people are doing? Are you reading *People* magazine and catching up on the latest celebrity gossip? Are you listening to music? OR are you reading something about your dreams, learning new things, listening to a podcast, writing your thoughts down or planning your next move?

If you want to be successful and rich at a young age, you have to collapse time frames. That only happens if you're CONSTANTLY working on becoming who you want to be. If you want to take a giant step towards achieving your dreams, get rid of your TV. Get rid of your screens.

It sets me off when people say they're bored. Are you kidding me? Have you achieved all you want in life? Are ALL your dreams fulfilled? Does your family have all they need? Have you done all that you can? If the answer is no, how could you possibly be bored? What you're experiencing isn't boredom, it's laziness. I've been guilty of it, too. It's easy to succumb to the many distractions and entertainments options.

The worst emotion to be caught up in is contentedness. Being content is the antithesis of making progress. We must be *ridiculously intentional* with what we choose to put into our mind. What we see and hear affects what we think. We now know that our thoughts ultimately determine what we get in life.

How badly do you want *what you say you want* in life? Enough to rid yourself of all the "noise" that doesn't move you closer to where you want to be? Enough to cancel cable? Enough to unplug your TV and your devices?

The average American watches three hours of TV a day! That's over 1,000 hours a year that each person devotes to filling his or her mind with stuff that adds no benefit other than the immediate gratification of not facing the real world.

Some people like to call it *relaxing*, when in reality, for many it's *escapism*. Don't get me wrong, there is a time for recovering from your exerted effort, for calming your mind and settling your anxiety; however, those things must be done with intention. Growth must be the continual pursuit.

NEWS FLASH: GREAT THINGS AREN'T ACCOMPLISHED BY CHILLIN'.

While I'm sure you're not one of those people who watch three hours of TV a day, you might be filling a lot of your time with *"chillin"*. If you're anything like who I was before I made radical changes, you're probably busy with video games, *SportsCenter* and the occasional Netflix binge. I speak so passionately about this subject because I was right there on the sofa with you.

Just think about how much time could be re-allocated to building your dream life or to accomplishing a small personal goal like losing seven pounds, or reading an entire book for once instead of just skimming through a few chapters.

Here's my challenge for you: unplug your TV for the next seven days. Every time you get the urge/thought/impulse to even go in front of the TV, stop and ask yourself, "What can I do right now that will move me closer to where I want to be in life?" DO THAT, DO IT NOW.

Journal your thoughts and log the time you spent working on whatever it is you chose to work on. Work through the empowering questions at the end of this chapter, analyze your limiting beliefs, look for mentors to help you along the way and read the rest of this book.

At the end of the week, you'll have momentum, and you'll be surprised to find out how much more productive you are. You would have trained your mind to think differently, and you'll be much closer to mastering your thoughts.

BECOME A MASTER *ASKER:* THE EMPOWERING QUESTIONS WORKSHEET

"Successful people ask better questions, and as a result, they get better answers."
-Tony Robbins

Great questions are questions that expand your mind and ultimately help you ask even greater questions. So, here's where the real work happens: empowering questions. Fill them out! Put these answers down on paper. They'll guide you towards the kind of mastery of your mind that's necessary for you to create success.

Note that these questions are formulated as things you can *do* rather than things you *can't do*. That simple transformation of language can completely change your worldview. The other thing you'll notice is that the questions are driven by the word *why*. *Why* is a question that gets to the root of things? When you plan, ask why and plan backwards from your goal to the steps you need to take to achieve it. Begin with the end in mind.

Use these questions to open up your mind rather than feel set on a one-way track.

What is the ideal/greatest version of myself? How would I describe this person?

_____

_____

_____

_____

_____

Why do I want this?

_____
_____
_____
_____
_____

What gives me my greatest feeling of importance? Nail it down to just one thing.

_____
_____
_____
_____
_____

Why does this thing give me that feeling?

_____
_____
_____
_____
_____

What are the Top 3 most important things in life to me?

1. _____
2. _____
3. _____

Imagine you're at the end of your life, lying on your deathbed, reflecting on your life. What did you accomplish before you pass away?

_____
_____
_____

What can I build that will afford me the lifestyle I want to live?

_____

_____

_____

_____

What do I want success to do for me?

_____

_____

_____

_____

_____

What do I want it to do for the world?

_____

_____

_____

_____

When life is going AMAZING and you're living your best life, what does it look like?

_____

_____

_____

_____

_____

What are the unwavering values with which I operate my life or my business?

1. _____

2. _____

3. _____

Is what I'm doing right now moving me closer or further away from my goals? (circle one)

YES / NO

What is the *one thing* I can do to make everything else easier?

_____

_____

_____

If you've taken the time to answer these questions, then I'll bet you feel empowered and ready to go. It's best to allow these questions and answers to simmer if you can. This is a good time to take a break and meditate on the answers you've come up with. Meditation doesn't mean sitting with your legs crossed and doing nothing. It means internalizing these questions and answers. Do some dishes, take a walk, jump in the shower, clean the house or run some errands while these questions steep in your subconscious.

Letting things soak in is a critical part of mastering your thoughts. Give your brain time to settle because that's where inspiration really comes through.

In the next chapter, you'll learn the value of mentorship and how to bring it into your life.

Resources:

Read: *Think and Grow Rich* by Napoleon Hill

Attend: A workshop, seminar, conference, retreat, etc. focused on personal development / mastering your mindset.

            Look for ways to add value to others.

**Download and complete the
"Empowering Questions" PDF worksheet here:**

https://seandgray.com/empoweringquestions_pdf

CHAPTER 2.
STEP 2 – GET A MENTOR

"If you want to get somewhere, it's best to find someone who's already been there."
- Robert Kiyosaki

Andy Tanner is Robert Kyosaki's paper asset advisor. I met Andy at a conference and he then invited me to one of his classes. During the class, he demonstrated something very interesting. He put a $20 bill on the table and as soon as he did, everybody in the room jumped to grab it. Andy looked at everyone, and he said, "You guys, that's pathetic. You're all grabbing for the money. That's why you're not rich."

You'd think just the opposite, right? We wanted that money more than anyone else, so that *should* make us rich, but that's not the case and Andy taught us a very important lesson.

He explained that the $20 on the table was not going to change our financial situation. We didn't want that money more than anyone else so we could make *more* of it; we wanted that money so we could spend it. We were all fighting over it. By jumping to grab it, we made the wrong choice.

That $20 did not have the power to change our lives because we've been conditioned to fight over it. For us, the value of that $20 was just that: $20. Maybe it was lunch. Maybe it was downtown parking for the day. Twenty dollars hardly even buys a movie ticket anymore.

But for someone who has the knowledge to convert an opportunity and maximize returns, that person would be able to get much more out of that $20.

For someone who could take that 20 bucks and invest it and then make 20 more, well that $20 bill wasn't a half-tank of gas. That $20 was the opportunity to keep making more and more money.

Andy pointed out that if we chose to capitalize on the opportunity that the $20 bill represented and instead invested it intelligently, we would be able to generate much higher returns from that $20. It is not the money that will change your financial situation, it is the financial knowledge you have that will change your financial situation - it is what you know to do with the money. For me, that was a polarizing experience.

No matter who you are, no matter what level of success you've achieved or have yet to achieve, you are going to find that without good guidance you're lost.

The people who consistently dominate in whatever they put their mind to have mentors. And the best of the best of have several mentors.

From world-class athletes to top business professionals, ALL elite individuals recognize and apply the power of a mentor. Imagine you never had anyone show you how to tie your shoes or ride a bike or how to drive a car. It would be extremely difficult and time-consuming to master those simple things on your own without any guidance, wouldn't it?

You'd most likely make quite a few costly and unnecessary mistakes. You'd get hurt. You'd run into a pole or tear up the gear shift. You'd skin your knees. You wouldn't get down the driveway. Imagine being on a sports team for the first time and not having a coach. Do you think you and your teammates would go out on the field of play in the first game and know exactly what's needed to win? Of course not.

The learning curve for everything in life is much longer and more costly without a mentor or coach. Learning is a community venture; it's something that comes through a partnership with others. It's not a solo act.

GREAT LEADERS HAVE MENTORS

Most great leaders of the world have relied on mentors.

"Education is the kindling of a flame, not the filling of a vessel."
—*Socrates*

Let's take it back to high school history class. Remember learning about Socrates, Plato, and Aristotle? These three classical thinkers shaped the way the Western world views itself and the way people interact with the rest of society. What I don't think most of us got in school was the powerful bond of mentorship.

Socrates was the first great thinker of the modern world, and he took on a student, Plato, and taught him his Socratic method. In case you've forgotten, the Socratic method is the way in which we investigate the world; the scientific method is based on it.

Plato revolutionized the way the world thought about the mind. He taught us how to think, and thanks in part to his teacher Socrates, he was able to shape the world that we know today. Our political system, the idea of freedom for all people, higher education, and the modern notions of ethical living can be traced back this one man. And then Plato took on a student of his own: Aristotle.

Aristotle is, in many ways, the founder of modern science. He also brought us the modern idea of virtue, of living life for the good of others. Logical thinking that laid the groundwork for everything from space travel to the stock market can be traced back to Aristotle.

Aristotle also took on his own student, a young boy who would one day be known as Alexander the Great. The modern world is here because of Alexander the Great. He expanded the Greek Empire further than any other leader in history. Alexander the Great is a model for young people because by the time he was 30 years old, he had created one of the largest empires in history, which stretched from Greece all the way to India. He was undefeated on the battlefield and was one of the most successful military commanders in all of history. The unification of culture that seems so normal today goes back to Alexander the Great. And he wasn't even 30 years old when he did it. He's considered one of the most influential people in history.

"I am indebted to my father for living. I am indebted to my teacher for living well."
–Alexander the Great

Why? Why was he able to do those amazing things at such a young age? He did it because he didn't start from zero.

Alexander the Great built his legacy by starting with a great mentor. It's because he learned at the feet of a master mentor, Aristotle, that he became who he was. Aristotle didn't start from zero either; he learned at the feet of his master, Plato. And, of course, Plato learned at the feet of his master, Socrates.

You can see examples of this principle in modern day. Look at modern-day, successful people. They all have incredible mentors. Tiger Woods' dad mentored him in golf from the time he was four years old. Kim Kardashian's mother, Kris Jenner mentored her in the ways of fame, and now Kim has built a massive financial empire that landed her on the cover of *Forbes*. I was mentored by my father, who gave me a leg up on my own journey. Find any person who is at the top of their industry or sport, and you'll find a mentor behind them who gave that person a head start.

Success, really big success, is too big for one lifetime. It has to be built upon the knowledge that's gained through years of experience. Generational knowledge is what propels the best people forward to greatness. Take advantage of the mentors in your life, and you'll be able to jump ahead by lifetimes.

WHAT IS A MENTOR?

A mentor is a person who has mastered the art of whatever it is you're setting out to do. A mentor is someone who has gone through the *mine field* already and will show you where to go and where not to go so you can achieve your desired outcome most efficiently.

It's been my good fortune to be on the receiving end of guidance from many great mentors in my life.

I've also been able to serve that function for some people who have become successful in their own right. As we've already seen, mentorship has a massive long-term impact on the lives of people. It's a life-changing experience.

From mentors, we learn how to be our own leaders. They don't provide us with specific instruction necessarily, but instead, they offer us the chance to grow into our best selves.

Here are some examples of what great mentors do.

- Challenge you.
- Encourage you to think through issues.
- Ask painfully difficult questions.
- Provide a source of wisdom.
- Feed you positive energy to propel you forward.

Though a mentor might only stay with us for a short time, the impact on us reverberates through the years. Mentors don't stay static. They continue to challenge us and keep us growing, even when they themselves fade into the background.

Having a good mentor will not only catapult you in the right direction and give you a major advantage but also will save you from several time-consuming, unnecessary and costly pitfalls. On top of that, a mentor has relationships and resources that you most likely want and need. Remember, it's all about building on the things that came before you. It's about that generational learning and taking advantage of the knowledge and experience of people who have already been there to allow you to reach success faster.

If you want to move quickly in the real world, follow a master mentor.

> *"A good coach is deaf at the right time - when I make excuses; blind at the right time - when all I see are road-blocks and forceful at the right time when I'm both blind and deaf."*
> *–Robert Kiyosaki*

A master mentor inspires you to act. It's someone you'd gladly trade places with – someone who has achieved success in the area in which you want to excel. A master mentor translates complex information in a way that you can easily understand and implement. This relationship is one you can count on; one you can take with you over the course of several years, not just for today.

Ideally, you want to be able to forge this relationship with an individual who can stick with you over time. It's an intimate relationship in many ways because it affects you deeply.

Keep in mind that the benefits of this relationship go both ways. You can get a lot out of the relationship from one end, but your Master Mentor is getting a great deal out of it as well. A mentor-mentee relationship is never one-sided.

HOW TO FIND A MASTER MENTOR

Having a mentor offers great benefits, but you can't take advantage of any of them if you don't know how to find that person who you need to help you shape your own destiny.

Let's start at the beginning: by changing the structure of your life. To find a mentor, you need to change your associations online and offline.

Surround yourself with people who are the best in the craft you're interested in and study them. Don't just study what they say, but study what they do. You can arguably learn more from them by watching them than you can by listening to what they say. There's truth in action. But you can't observe the behavior of people if you're surrounded by those who aren't inspiring to you. In short, to be the best, you must associate with the best.

"Surround yourself with only people who are going to lift you higher."
–Oprah Winfrey

Reach out to others who are going in the same direction as you. Engage with people who are where you want to be. As you start getting out there and talking to people who have been where you are, you'll be surprised to find many opportunities coming your way. These opportunities will propel you toward your current goals.

A major part of this process is getting outside your comfort zone. You'll have to go to conferences, gatherings, events, meetings, and more to connect with these kinds of people. You're not going to find a mentor sitting on your couch or from your phone. You'll even find it challenging to find a mentor on social media. If you want to find the right mentor, you need to get out there and actually be social. Go out to the places where these people are. Connection is everything, and you'll know when you find the mentor who resonates with you. Remember, most ventures in life are more enjoyable when pursued with other like-minded and passionate people.

WHY WOULD A MENTOR INVEST IN ME?

Successful people typically want to help others.

"I can get all I want in life if I just help enough other people get what they want."
-Zig Ziglar

Mentors have internalized Zig Ziglar's famous quote. Even more so, mentors want to help those who want to be helped AND those who take action towards their dreams.

Have you ever coached someone, maybe in a sport, and then they implemented what you taught them and made a great play? It's that same feeling you got watching them make the play that compels many mentors to give generously. Mentors share in the feeling of success that their mentees create. That's a powerful thing. Simply, success breeds success. When a mentor helps move a mentee progress, they often experience connected success and progress.

Some people will say, "But a professional mentor costs too much." My question is: *costs too much* compared to what? Compared to the costly and time-sucking mistakes you're likely to make alone? From my experience, the cost of ignorance is far more expensive and certainly more time consuming than the investment in mentors.

"But, Sean, I honestly can't afford mentorship right now."
I get it but that thought is exactly one of the thought patterns we need to fix.

Instead of saying, "I can't afford it", give your mind a better problem to solve and ask, "How can I afford it?" then let your extremely powerful subconscious to go to work on it. You'll be surprised at some of the ideas that come to you.

Furthermore, paying money for mentorship isn't the only way to get it. Uncovering what the person you want to build a relationship with wants, needs and desires can be just as valuable, if not more so, than money. In every successful relationship value is exchanged. Find the value your potential mentors want or need and then find a way to provide it. We'll get more into the skill it takes to master this in Step 6.

Nonetheless, wherever you're at, I encourage you to find mentors. Whether in-person or virtual mentors - read their books, listen to their podcasts, attend their seminars, webinars, workshops, and join their communities. When given the opportunity, ask great questions! Then implement the advice your mentor gives you. Knowledge without action is useless. And nothing will turn a mentor off more than not heeding their advice.

MY MENTOR EXPERIENCES

I've been lucky enough to have enriching mentor relationships in my life. To help you understand more deeply the way this has worked for me, I'm going to share with you some of my own mentoring experiences.

Financial Author and Rich Dad - Robert Kiyosaki

One of the best-selling financial authors of all time, Robert Kiyosaki had been someone I'd followed for some time before I got the chance to meet with him.

I was privileged to meet him at the Investor Summit at Sea, and had some incredible conversations with him that helped propel me forward to success.

He helped me understand that the rich don't work for money. They allow their money to work for them. That perspective is revolutionary for most of us. Being right there with someone that has lived that in real life allowed me to see that path in my own life. In a conversation with him on a private boat in St. Marteen, he told me, *"What got me here is not going to be what gets me to the next level."*

At that moment, I realized that he and I aren't different at all and the process truly never ends. I saw myself reflected in this man because he was where I wanted to be. But what really resonated with me was his concept that got me to where I am. I wasn't going to get to the next level on my own without him. Though I may be at a different point in my life path than him, I can still see that he's reaching for the next level with the same yearning that I am. That's the power of mentorship.

Sales Trainer - Tom Hopkins

Iconic sales trainer Tom Hopkins made an incredible impression on me. His book, *How to Master the Art of Selling*, had already been formative for me in terms of my understanding of how to harness my interactions with other people and deal with rejection. To spend time with him in person and have access to his knowledge and experience firsthand was more than powerful.

He showed me why it's important to be a mentor. He told me how amazing it was to see students internalize what you'd taught them, then to watch them go on and have great success.

It was through my work with Tom that I learned to understand why people become mentors, why that work is so fulfilling. That knowledge allowed me to embrace my role as a mentor because I knew that it wasn't a one-way street. The mentor-mentee relationship is one that's a win-win. It's great for everyone. That same view is one that Tom carries into all his dealings.

The other thing I learned from Tom is that failure is something we can only view as a learning experience; an opportunity to develop our sense of humor.

*"I never view failure as failure, but only as an opportunity to grow and improve." -**Tom Hopkins***

Finally, I learned from Tom to more effectively structure my day with morning mental workout chants. This simple addition to my days allowed me to be more productive and focused throughout the day and to waste less time and to go forward more effectively. Sometimes the best things we learn from mentors are the smallest.

The Real Estate Guys – Robert Helms and Russell Gray

Sometimes mentors come in pairs. That was the case for me when I found myself working with Robert Helms and Russell Gray, the Real Estate Guys.

The core lesson I learned from them was about building strong relationships.

These men worked together to create a massively successful brand through real estate investment education.

Remember earlier when I said you needed to find people who were doing what you wanted to do? That's exactly what these two did. They were focused on goal setting and relationship building through those common goals. I found out that connections could be the best part of this process, better than even the financial benefits.

There's clarity to the philosophy of Robert and Russell. They work for clear goals that lead them towards positive outcomes. It's through them that I learned to develop my PIP (Personal Investment Philosophy). Financials aren't a cold, hard, cookie cutter thing; they're actually incredibly self-focused and individualized. These two guys taught me that you have to make this path your own, and so I was able to make it my own.

Founder of Jim Rohn Int. – Kyle Wilson

Kyle Wilson turned out to be an inroad for me to learn about creating networks. Success isn't a straight line; it's a web of connections you get to climb up toward a goal. The marvelously successful marketing of Jim Rohn had long been an example to me, but until I worked with Kyle, I didn't know how to leverage those ideas in my own spheres.

Leveraging the strengths of other people and other experts is exactly what Kyle does best. That's not taking advantage of anyone; it's simply raising the water level to a point where all boats float higher. Kyle has learned to leverage brands outside of his own to pull everyone up, and it's a strategy that's a win-win for all people involved.

My time as his mentee guided me to a more foundational understanding of what it means to be a part of a group; to be a part of something bigger.

Real Estate Mogul and Rich Dad Advisor – Ken McElroy

Occasionally, we get to have mentor experiences with people at the top of the business, and those are the best experiences we can have. I've been able to work closely with Ken McElroy and early on in our relationship I asked him, "What is the number one thing I can do today to move me closer to my goals in life and closer to financial freedom?"

Without a moment's hesitation, he answered with a deafeningly simple response: "Change the people you're around."

A huge reason you're reading this book right now is because of Ken. He's the one who encouraged me to focus on building a community of young ambitious individuals. He's the one who helped me see where my talents and experience would best be served, and that's through sharing what I've learned. Sometimes people change the course of your life. This was one of those times for me. I'm hoping that the domino effect means that it leads to being one of those times for you as well.

Sovereign Man– Simon Black

Finding mentors often means planning far into the future. Attending Simon Black's Blacksmith Liberty and Entrepreneurship camp in Lithuania had always been on my goal list. In fact, it was so important that I wrote a statement proclaiming I would attend his camp – signed and dated – and hung up on my wall in front of my desk. In August of 2014, although thousands of students applied, I was selected as one of the 50 students to attend this exclusive event. Coincidence?

I think not. We'll talk more about how I made that happen later on.

This event was nothing short of phenomenal. Simon's focus on personal liberty, paired with the understanding of personal liberty and exposure to how economies, countries, and ultimately the real-world works, was mind blowing and eye opening. I learned that the core principle of freedom is the basis of true capitalism and entrepreneurship. Simon showed me the bigger picture of what this is all about, the larger view of our ability to impact the world at large and the people that are close to us.

Humanity will always overcome everything else. Entrepreneurs are the ones who change the world. Young people today in particular, have a huge opportunity because of where we are at in history. The question is whether we're willing to take that chance or if we want to continue to stay in the background. The answer is that we do want to take our place in history. We just have to be brave enough to do it.

@nerdgonerogue - Katriel Sarfati

Go ahead and put the book down for a second and go follow @nerdgonerogue on Instagram ... you can thank me later.

It's some of the best content on Insta. That's the account of a brilliant marketing mind and someone who I started out a fan of then found a way to get into a relationship with and now someone I talk with on a regular basis on ways to grow my brand, my business and gain clarity on what to do next.

I admired Katriel and the content he would share from behind my phone for a couple years before getting in contact with him. I would study not just his content, but also how he delivered it, when he delivered it and dissected who he was talking to and why. Of course, I engaged with his content, commented, shared, etc. Then after feeling like I knew what he was all about, I contacted him and asked if I could interview and promote him. Who doesn't want more promotion?

He said yes, and we ended up having a virtual video interview which led to a much longer conversation offline, which then turned into us connecting in person and brainstorming on how we could help each other grow.

As our relationship developed, I began to realize how much of an impact Katriel was having on me. He was changing the way I thought about marketing and more specifically, how to connect with my audience in the most authentic way possible.

See, Katriel doesn't segment people on demographics like most marketing gurus or businesses. Instead, he focuses on psychographics. What is the person I'm trying to connect with experiencing and feeling? Why do they believe they're in the situation they're in? What are they hoping to become? What are they saying to themselves?

These are the types of questions he explores and ultimately what he bases his content and copy on. And because he does that, he's able to connect with people in a REAL way. He's able to meet people where they're at in life with empathy and show them he understands their problem, sees their vision, and because of that, is able to better help them become what they want to become.

Remember, people will be loyal to you in direct proportion to the amount of personal growth they experience as a result of you being in their life. Although Katriel doesn't necessarily consider himself a 'salesperson', it's this type of approach that is the basis of great sales (something we'll talk more about later on) and what caused me to want to share Katriel with you in this book.

As you can see, I haven't had just one Mentor in my professional life – I've had many and continue to build relationships with new ones. Each of these relationships has helped me to build my life into the thing that I wanted it to be. I'm so much better for having forged these mentor relationships. The trick is to catch the opportunity to learn from a master whenever you can.

YOUR MENTORS – WORKSHEET

Now it's time for you to take all of this and boil it down for yourself. You've already had mentor relationships in your life. Processing those will help you to seek out positive mentor relationships for the future.

What are two mentor relationships that you've had that meant something to you? They can be in any area.

1. _____
2. _____

What are the top 3-5 most important lessons that you learned (distinctions, ideas, resources) from each mentor that helped you accelerate your path to success?

1. _____
   a. _____
   b. _____
   c. _____
   d. _____
   e. _____

2. _____

a. _____

b. _____

c. _____

d. _____

e. _____

Now for some action steps.

Research and record three ways that you're going to try to connect with mentors through the online world. These can be mentors that you want to start following, online groups to connect with and websites to check out.

1. _____

2. _____

3. _____

Now for mentorship in the real world.

Look for three live, in-person events that you want to attend in the next year to connect with mentors. They can be local or far afield; it doesn't matter.

1. Name _____
Time and Date _____
Place _____

2. Name _____
Time and Date _____
Place _____

3. Name _____
Time and Date _____
Place _____

In the next chapter, we'll dig deeper into how to surround yourself with other people, just like you, who are motivated, ambitious and on the fast-track to success.

We'll expand on where you can go to find mentors and supportive peers, how you can make the transition to better relationships, and how you can get yourself motivated to make all of this happen.

Read: *Rich Dad Poor Dad* by Robert Kiyosaki

Attend: A conference, tradeshow, workshop or seminar on a topic or industry you want to know more about.

Download & Complete
"Your Mentors" PDF worksheet here:
https://seandgray.com/yourmentors_pdf

Look for the best and most successful people in the place and watch them. Look and listen for an opportunity to add value to that person or someone who influences that person.

CHAPTER 3.
STEP 3. CHANGE THE PEOPLE YOU'RE AROUND

"We are like chameleons; we take our hue and the color of our moral character, from those who are around us."
- John Locke

The quotation by John Locke refers to moral character and how we tend to behave like the people around us. However, when it comes to success, investment and growing your money, nothing is more important than surrounding yourself with the right people.

Success can only be achieved if you learn from the best. How can you learn from the best? By being around the best. It's as simple as that.

I always say that success is greatly dependent on how we think; what our thought process is; how we perceive things. One of the most critical elements of success is the ability to master your thoughts and have the courage to change the way you think. Why? Because you cannot achieve any success without change. Change is the way you grow.

Change is your pathway to new avenues and greener pastures. If you don't change; if you limit yourself, you can hardly expect to achieve big things and reach newer destinations.

Let's look at it this way. When we are in college, we study theories and concepts. We learn the textbook version of life. And that has its value, no doubt. We need this foundation to guide us as we set out to achieve our true path. But the protective world of your classroom is vastly different from the real world.

If you want to be successful, understand the process of making a transition from college. Be prepared to switch from a structured way of life to something that is more fragmented and broken. Move from textbook thinking patterns and adopt a new way of thinking that will help you stay afloat in the real world; a world dramatically different from your textbooks.

If you want to be successful in this world, change the way you think. How do you achieve that? You can achieve that by changing the people around you. Think of it this way. Does anybody ever really teach you your natural language? We do have to learn certain concepts – grammar, punctuation, pronunciation, etc. but does anybody ever really sit down with you and teach you your language? No, not really. That's because we are surrounded by people who speak the same language. If English is your parent's first language, you learn to speak English even before you're in Kindergarten. Similarly, if French is your parent's first language, you will be speaking French as soon as you can talk.

The same concept applies to money. You can learn to invest it the right way by interacting with people who are well-versed and knowledgeable about money and investments. Remember that no matter which professional career you choose, you have to keep in mind you were not born into that profession. To become a master in that particular field, learn from people who know what you don't know. In simple words, Step 3 is all about changing the way you think by surrounding yourself with masters of their craft.

Keep in mind that when I say transition, I don't mean a simple physical transition from a college classroom to an office in Wall Street. I am talking about making an emotional transition; a mental transition. I am talking about preparing yourself for highs and lows and successes and failures.

You will not reach the top as soon as you begin. If you want to succeed, surround yourself with masters. By surrounding yourself with masters, you can make the process of transition easier for yourself.

Transitioning from one point to another is an inevitable reality of our lives. We can't get ahead if we don't transition. We can't move forward if we're not willing to change. Believe me, I speak from personal experience.

Up until a few years ago, I was a football player. I had big dreams of playing in the NFL. I worked very very hard to achieve this goal. When I was 11 years old, I was playing with a team called the Wildcats. Many of my friends were on this team so I was very comfortable with my surroundings. I was also a major contributor to the success of my team.

However, one year our team did not have enough kids that signed up to play and we could not meet the 16-man minimum roster requirement. That meant we could not participate in the league. Each of us now had a choice: we could either split up and join other teams, or we could stick together and combine rosters with one other team. Here was the moment of transition, the moment of change.

This point of transition was difficult for me for two reasons. If I chose the second option, I knew that the other team sucked. They were also 45 minutes from my house. If I decided to go with the first option, I could join a team called the Red Devils. At that time, they were three-time defending national champions – the best team in the country. Keep in mind that I was 12 years old at the time. It was a big, big decision for me.

What should I do? Stay with my friends and surround myself with people who I was comfortable with where I could be a big fish in a small pond or join the reigning champions, the popular Red Devils and be a small fish in a big pond?

It was a challenging time; a difficult transition. I was in my comfort zone. I was with my friends. I was surrounded by people who I knew very well. Was I ready for a change? Was I ready to leave them behind to pursue my dreams?

My dad asked me what I wanted to do and the first answer that came to my mind was that I wanted to stay with my friends. At that point, my dad asked me what my goals were as far as football was concerned, and again, I had no hesitation in saying that I wanted to play in the NFL and become the best football player ever. Do you know what he said to me?

He said, "*If you want to be the best, you have to compete with the best.*" And that, my friends, is principle number one.

If I wanted to be the greatest football player ever, I had to leave my friends, my comfort zone, my hard-earned reputation and my position. I had to leave it all behind, and I had to find the courage to make the transition into a completely new territory; a territory where I did not know anyone and where I was likely going to be a small fish initially.

The choice was clear. If I wanted to be best, I had to start playing with the best. So, I decided to join the Red Devils.

That same year, I earned a starting spot on the Red Devils, led my new team in interceptions, and we went on to become the National Champions. Only one other player on my previous team decided to play with the best. And incidentally, we were the only two of the three players from the Wildcats team who went on to play college football.

I did not make it to the NFL but I did play longer and higher than 97% of kids who play football, plus the other kid that went on to play in the NFL from my team. How did this happen?

This happened because I chose to surround myself with people who were the best. By playing with the best, I became better and better, and I went further than nearly every player from that Wildcats team. The point is that if you want to be successful in your particular field or segment, you have to immerse yourself in an environment with people who are far more advanced than you.

Now I want you to understand that I am not undervaluing friends and family. I had to give up playing with my friends, but that does not mean I gave up my friends. It is important to be able to distinguish your personal relationships from your professional ones.

It is important to know which masters you need to surround yourself with to become your own master. I once asked one of my mentors, *"What is the number one thing I can do to better myself and move closer towards my goals?"* He answered without hesitation, *"Change the people you're around."*

When you think about it, this advice is both logical and simple. If you want to learn how to work on cars, you wouldn't ask a massage therapist now, would you? Obviously not. What you would do to become skilled with cars would be to work with people who are very skillful with cars. In my experience, you become the sum total of the five people you spend the most time around. Now think: if you want to excel in something, doesn't it make sense to spend time with people who are where you would want to be, if not ahead? Of course, it does.

Always try to surround yourself with people who are better at doing what you want to do. Like they say, "*You never want to be the smartest guy in the room.*" Why? Because if you're already the smartest, you can't learn from the people around you. If you surround yourself with people who are better, you will become better too.

Now the question is: how do you know you're spending time with the right people?

How can you be sure? Well, you can determine that by asking yourself the following questions:

- What is important to you?
- What lifestyle do you want to live?
- Who do you want to be?

These questions help you define your value hierarchy. In other words, you will be able to gain a clear understanding of what your values are. Once you know this, it will become easier for you to identify who you should and shouldn't be spending time with. And when you identify these people, try to find every opportunity you can to be with them. Attend events, seminars, and workshops with like-minded people. Maximize the benefits of face-to-face interaction. I know in this age of the Internet and technology, everybody seems to be communicating online but, in my opinion, face to face interaction is the fastest way to form and develop long-term and successful relationships. Remember, they always say, it's not about 'what' you know, but 'who' you know and 'how' they know you that matters the most.

So, if you want to succeed, you need to apply these three key principles:

1. Change the way you think by mastering your thoughts.

2. Follow a mentor and try to learn from people who have already advanced much further than you and who have mastered their craft.

3. Surround yourself with masters in the making which includes people who are headed in the same direction or those who are where you want to be.

Adopt and apply these principles consistently. This is a continuous process. You won't achieve success in a day. You will experience highs and lows; You will see both success and failure. You will experience optimism and defeat. You will sometimes be scared; sometimes be confident.

You will feel and experience multiple emotions; this is part of the real world. It is a reality. You will not become a master in a day but you will develop the power to master the real world. When you develop this power, you will be more successful in the real world.

Once again, I want to clarify that I am not propagating separation from people you love and people who matter. What I am recommending is to develop the ability to distinguish between relationships that allow you to thrive and relationships that hold you back. Sometimes it's necessary to change the dynamic of certain relationships. Legendary sales trainer Tom Hopkins taught me to never take advice from anyone more messed up than I am. I stopped taking financial advice from people who weren't in a financial situation better than me. Similarly, I stopped taking relationship advice from people who didn't have the type of relationships I wanted, and so on. This makes perfect sense because if you want to succeed, you need to listen to and take advice from people who are better than you, not equal to or worse.

It is important to apply this principle. You need to be around people who are successful and who are masters in their field. However, you should never let your circle of influence hold you back from being the person you want to be. This is very, very important. This is not just relevant to your professional life but also your personal life. Why do you think so many relationships fail? Do you think it is because you just made a wrong choice? No.

Relationships fail because when we fall in love or make a commitment with someone at a certain point in our lives, we expect that love and commitment to remain the same for the rest of our lives. But that is impossible. That is impossible because there is no constant in life except for change. Change is inevitable. Change is necessary. You cannot grow without change. You can't put somebody in a box and expect them to stay the same forever. If you do that, you are limiting their growth, and when you limit somebody's growth, there can only be two possible outcomes. Either they, at some point, break and so does the relationship or they stay in the box you've placed them in and end up resenting you.

They compromise and live a life of regret and what-ifs. There is no point in being in such a relationship.

There is a quote from Jim Rohn which really suits this concept. *"The greatest gift you can give to someone is your own personal development."* Instead of expecting others to behave in a certain manner or live with you in a certain manner, you should focus on developing yourself. If you take care of yourself and let others take care of their own growth, both parties will benefit and the relationship, whether personal or professional, will flourish and be more successful.

You can understand the damage a person can incur if they are held back by putting yourself in their shoes.

Would you be happy if somebody holds you back? No. Would you be happy if somebody expected you to behave in a certain manner even though you didn't want to behave that way? No.

Then why do we expect others to be a certain way? The way we want them to be? People will change when they are ready to change. You cannot force change. Yes, you can give them the opportunity to change. You can help facilitate that change.

But you cannot make that change happen till they want to change. The point is that you need to focus on yourself. You need to find mentors. You need to soak yourself in inspiration. You need to learn from the best to be the best and ultimately change your thinking. Doing these things will dramatically impact your transition into the real world.

Resources:

Read: *How To Win Friends And Influence People* by Dale Carnegie

Attend: Or host a mastermind, book study, or meetup around something you're passionate about or personal development of some kind.

Look for ways to add value to others.

CHAPTER 4.
MAKING THE
TRANSITION

"A transition period is a period
between two transition periods."
–George Stigler

In the last few chapters, we covered changing the way we do things, changing the people around us, and getting ourselves mentors. You have to be prepared that when you're in the process of making these changes and when you're making the transition, you might feel lost or unsure. Be prepared to feel this way and be open to the challenges and the experiences you're likely to have during this process of transition. If you're not prepared for the emotions and growing pains you're about to experience, you almost most certainly will succumb to them and impede your growth dramatically.

Change is difficult to handle for most people. Even if it's a positive change, it does take some time for us to adjust to the new "reality." Some examples include transitioning from Junior High to High School or from High School to College or transitioning from one job to another, we tend to get accustomed to a certain structure. It's as if somebody has scripted our entire life for us – what we will do, where we will live, where we will go and even sometimes what we will wear.

And suddenly you're in transition mode, and everything seems to be in limbo. Your subconscious will suddenly start to look for something familiar to latch onto.

This will happen and when it does, don't be surprised or shocked. It's a natural process of transition. You may feel as if you're adrift; you may search for that familiar structure but if you don't find it, don't panic. In fact, it's a good thing because real-world exposure and real-world experience are now part of your new reality – they are your next level of education, and the sooner you become aware of this and accept it, the smoother the transition will be.

One of the best ways to successfully make a transition is not to make any long-term commitments. By that, I don't mean you should never take anything seriously. What I do mean is that you should not make any long-term commitments that put limits on your growth before you have enough exposure and experience, before you are sure you can fulfill those commitments and more importantly, before you are sure it's really what you want to be attached to.

For example, if you take on a project or if you accept a job, make sure you know what you're getting yourself into. Don't just accept it because you want money or because you have bills to pay. Again, I'm not undermining the importance of money or income here.

What I'm trying to say is that you should never commit to doing something simply for the money. If you do take a job, take it for the experience you'll gain and the relationships you'll develop.

I understand if someone has to accept a certain task because they have to stay afloat; they have to pay the rent; they have to buy groceries; this makes perfect sense.

But do keep in mind that while a job can provide income, it can also trap you in an employee mindset. Have a bigger vision than just what is in front of you.

I always tell people to keep their options open while also knowing which things to say 'no' to. When you bind yourself in a typical structure, you tend to close yourself to opportunities. You get a job; you start getting a regular paycheck. You then buy a car; you get a mortgage and so on. What have you done? You've actually increased your liabilities, and these are the liabilities that are likely to keep you trapped within this routine and this structure.

That is what I mean by not committing yourself to something that is not the highest vision for yourself.

We tend to take on new debts because we have money coming in. This is called your MPC or your marginal propensity to consume – the more money you make, the more money you spend. It's natural. Be aware of this. If routine is how you thrive, have a routine, but be cautious to not fall into a comfort zone. But keep moving in a direction where you continue to learn and grow. This way you can kill two birds with one stone – you will be able to pay the bills, but you will also remain on the fast track to build the ultimate lifestyle you desire.

I understand that we are trained throughout our lives to earn money. That seems to be the end-all and be-all for most people. But it's not about the money.

It's about success. If you think that money is what determines your success, I encourage you to go back and read the previous chapters again.

Running after money is a trap that we all tend to fall into, and yes, you do need money to survive, but it is not the end goal - and that is the slippery slope. Working strictly for accumulating money will make you a slave to it.

I am not saying don't accept that job. I'm not saying don't get that degree. Do everything that you believe in, but do it with awareness. Don't pigeonhole yourself. Don't make long-term commitments.

Don't accumulate a huge amount of debt. Remember, you already have that student loan to pay off (at least most of you do). You don't want to burden yourself with more debt. Don't rely too much on that job of yours because you still require more real-world exposure and more real-world experience. That's the only way you will succeed in the long-run. Don't limit yourself without gaining all that experience and without understanding the real world completely. If you keep your options open, you will eventually be able to determine what you really want to do.

You know when we get to high school, it feels as if we've just been given a fresh start. We get an opportunity to start over; rebuild our reputation; create a new image etc. When we get into college, it's the same kind of feeling, especially for those who go into a new town or city. It's a new experience. Getting into the real world is really quite similar to this feeling.

The real world is your next big opportunity – the next big chunk. You can rebrand yourself; you can build your image and reputation. It's a transition from what you were before to what you will be in the next phase of your life.

I still remember the transition phase that I went through when I went to college. In those days, football was everything to me. When I went to college, it was a new football team. I did not know anyone there but that did not scare me. I looked at it as an opportunity.

I could have any persona on the field because nobody knew me there and so they couldn't differentiate between who I was before and whom I wanted to be now.

Obviously, my experience in high school had given me a certain insight as to whom I wanted to be in college. At my new college and with my new team, I wanted to brand myself as somebody who had a lot of confidence. I wanted to come across as somebody with a lot of swagon the field; a lot of courage. That's just how I chose to brand myself as football was my focus. During this transition phase and this rebranding process, I learned a lot of things. I learned how to handle the transition. I learned how to rebrand myself continuously.

There are two important things you need to do to make it through a transition: determine what brand you want to build and start building it right away. Don't think of this as your last opportunity. Think of it as a new opportunity; the next phase of your life. Think of it as the opportunity you can use to build the foundation for who you really want to be.

I know transitioning can be very hard. Do you know why? It's because we all become accustomed to living in a certain way. It's like we become part of a system and we're on a certain track. It's a comfortable position to be in. You have everything laid out. You know where you are and you know where you're probably going to go.

And then we go and change our direction or take on a new path and suddenly our system freaks out. We feel lost and uneasy.

This is completely natural so don't think you're the only one who wants to latch on to the old system. We all go through the same thing when we transition from one point to another. But the one thing that can make your transition easier is if you don't make long-term commitments; if you don't become too dependent on that job; if you don't accumulate too much debt. In other words, if you don't become too comfortable with where you are today.

When you are young, you still have time to brand and rebrand yourself. You can transform yourself multiple times. You can redesign your lifestyle. You can look at the big picture. But if you limit yourself and focus on only one thing, you can't go much further. We all get trapped in the same routine because that's what we've been trained to do. Everybody tells us we must study and find a good job. But nobody tells us that we should also spread our wings and keep our options open. Everybody wants stability; nobody wants growth and expansion.

Here's how many of us fall into the trap of money: Our subconscious is powerful and we are constantly but often unaware of the suggestions we tell our brain.

When we graduate, we ask ourselves, *"What do I do now to make money?"* This is a completely logical question because that's the way we've been raised.

But if you think about it, this question is what leads you into a trap that you cannot get out of. When we ask ourselves how we can make money, it makes money the end goal. And it makes the path to get that money by "doing" something – exchanging time and effort for that money.

A better question to ask yourself is, *"What can I build that will afford me the lifestyle that I want to live?"* This makes lifestyle your end goal, and instead of "exchanging your time and effort" as the means to get there, you are now building something of your own. Build something for yourself instead of just doing something. Both approaches require work but if you work on building your lifestyle, there will be a point where the thing you built will afford you freedom.

Learn to approach the process of transition with an open mind. Don't think of transition as something that will complicate your system; that will shake your foundation. Think of transition as the way to build yourself further.

I understand that you might feel lost. But when you feel lost, try to revisit your vision. The best way to overcome that lost feeling is clarity of vision.

Once you're clear about who you want to be and the lifestyle you want to live, the steps to get there will automatically become evident.

Whenever I was stuck in that lost feeling, my dad would tell me, *"With clarity of vision, strategy and tactics become evident."* And that made a lot of sense to me.

You might ask how you can gain this clarity. We'll talk about this more when we come to Step 5 in this process. However, it ultimately comes down to designing your ideal lifestyle and setting goals within it.

Patience is required in the beginning when making a transition. By patience I mean the patience to understand the challenges and the changes this transition will bring. I don't mean you should be slow to grab the opportunities. For that, you do need to have a sense of urgency.

Evaluate your life for a moment. How fast did your high school years go by? How fast did you get through college? Real life is going to be even faster. Nobody will wait for you to catch up. Everybody is running after something, and if you lag behind, you're going to lose your place. Don't think you have a lot of time because you don't. So... always be patient with the challenges a transition brings but live with a sense of urgency. Life is short. Don't waste it. Dream big and work diligently to realize those dreams.

Your biggest advantage is that you're still young. People often think being young is a disadvantage. But I think otherwise. In fact, I believe this is the best time to be a young entrepreneur. You have so many technological tools to take advantage of. You have the largest millennial workforce at your disposal. And best of all, you have all those experienced, wise and successful people around you who could be your mentors.

You're young. Your part of an era where advancement is an everyday thing. You have tools these people never had, and still, they got where they are today. Learn from them, apply what you learn and make it better because you're young. You have ambition. You have energy. You have drive. And you have the right tools. Leverage that. Remember that the right mentors will want to help you. They want to see you succeed. And if you follow them and if you capitalize on your ambition, you will succeed.

Prepare yourself for one thing. When you're on the lookout for opportunities; when you've decided to explore your options and realize your vision, that is when you will get many opportunities. People will come to you with great ideas. They will present attractive opportunities and tempting deals. They will offer you lucrative positions in their company. Believe me, when you open yourself to opportunities, you will get chances that you never expected.

But this is the part where you have to handle things with awareness. Just because you can, doesn't always mean you should.

Just because you're getting many opportunities does not mean you should grasp them all. Don't be impatient here. Think long and hard. Think about your end goal. Think about the outcome. Think about the why and the where. Just because you have an opportunity does not mean you should take it. You should take it only if you believe that it will take you closer to where you want to be in life. Ask yourself: *"Does this opportunity move me closer to my goals? Is it a great opportunity for me and what I'm trying to do, what I'm trying to get, and most importantly who I want to be?"*

While we're talking about opportunities here, there's another thing to consider. You also have to prepare yourself for times when things are not so rosy. In every phase of life, we have ups and downs; peaks and valleys. There will be times when you will feel as if you're on top of the world and then there will be times when you will feel like a complete failure.

You will feel stuck. You will feel as if you're moving too slowly; as if you're too far away from your goal. But you have to understand that highs and lows are part of life. That's the way life goes. When you're at your low point, you must stay strong. You cannot get emotional at this time.

One of the most important traits of a successful businessperson is their ability to separate emotions when making decisions. Blair Singar taught me that when emotions run high, intelligence runs low.

It's never as bad as it seems and it's never as good as it seems. You have to use your head, especially during the tough times. You have to understand that in life, it is important to maintain balance. Everything is cyclical. The peaks and valleys. The highs and lows. The excitement and the frustration. That's what makes life exciting.

When you're high, keep your feet on the ground and continue to learn and grow. When you're low, focus on your goal and work on the things that you can control. And what are the two main things you can control? Your attitude and your effort. As long as you can sustain these two elements, there is no force on earth that can stop you from succeeding.

The real struggle that most entrepreneurs go through is getting through the highs and lows.

It's like you're pushing the boulder uphill. Sometimes, it's easy and the boulder rolls smoothly and you barely have to push, but at other times, it feels that you have to put in everything that's inside of you to stop the boulder from rolling backward and crushing you. You can think of it as an iterative process, one you have to learn to master. This is what transition is all about. Nothing is ever permanent.

Things will keep on changing but as long as your efforts are consistent and your attitude is positive, you will survive.

Whenever I felt that things were out of my control or the process was fuzzy, my dad would say, *"Build your brand. Build your network."* Why? Because it's always something you can do. When you are able to build a powerful brand, it is that power that will have your network presenting new opportunities to you and give you the opportunity for more clarity.

The key thing to remember here is that your brand is you. It's who you are. It's how you talk. It's how you dress. It's how you carry yourself. It's the way people feel about you after they're done talking to you. To get through the process of transition, you will have to build and rebuild your brand. And while you build your brand, you will also need to build your network and build your relationships. It's not about what you know. It's about who you know and how they know you. So, get out there. Meet people. Let them get to know you and get to know them. When you're transitioning, the most important thing you need to do is to keep learning and building.

Socrates said, *"When you're breaking an old habit, don't focus on breaking the old habit, but focus on forming the new habit."* If you want to learn how to make the transition, you need to learn how to break old habits.

Don't focus on what you don't want to do. Focus on what you want to do. Don't think about the negatives. Think about the opportunity that transitioning from Point A to Point B is presenting to you. Grab that opportunity. Take it positively. Learn to grow through the transition.

If you don't master transition, you not only limit your growth but become a slave to your current situation and current level of personal mastery.

Resources:

Read: *Turning Pro* by Steven Pressfield

Attend: Or host a mastermind, book study, or meetup around something you're passionate about or personal development of some kind.

Look for ways to add value to others.

CHAPTER 5.
STEP 4 –THE 'REAL WORLD' EXPOSED

"It is well enough that people of the nation do not understand our banking and monetary system, for if they did, I believe there would be a revolution before tomorrow morning."
– Henry Ford

I humbly ask that you forget everything you think you know about money. It is highly likely you've never been taught financial education. Or the little financial knowledge you have gained was probably instilled in you from a young age by your parents and how the people around you interacted with money based off their experiences. But there is a truth about what money actually is and how it affects your life. There are facts about our monetary system that will make you a slave to the dollar if you don't understand them.

This chapter is written with the purpose of opening your eyes to those truths. Keep in mind; however, if I were to go into the full extent of our monetary structure and the full nature of money and currency, this book would be thousands of pages. Instead what I will do here is explain crucial concepts to get you started down the path of mastering money.

Again, this book is not a get rich quick blueprint, it is a guide so you must continue to study this imperative topic on your own, as I still do to this day, and I will share resources that will expand on the information shared here.

In the first chapter we talked about changing your mindset about life and money. And that truly is where money is made – in your head. You'll find it to be even easier to do that when you discover some truths about money.

First, you need to understand that there was a purposeful reason why you were never taught these things in school. There are three types of education – formal, professional and financial. Formal education is your schooling – pre-school through college. Professional education would come if you decided to study to become a doctor or lawyer or some specialized field. Financial education isn't taught in an institution, but it is arguably the most important of the three. After all, you go through formal and professional education to hopefully get a job that pays you money.

But with no financial education, the money you gain will be highly taxed, hard earned in terms of time invested and even harder to keep and grow. The reason why financial knowledge isn't taught is because the elite do not want everyone to be rich; it would minimize their control. You'll start to see why as this chapter continues.

Furthermore, John D. Rockefeller designed the school system during the Industrial Age – a time when America needed trained workers for the factory productions.

The entire system was designed to make employees who were able to communicate with and work for the wealthy, but never become them.

And if you haven't noticed yet, or you recall the concepts in the introduction, you know that generally a job, or working for someone else is not the fastest or best way to become wealthy or live on your own terms.

So, what do you need to know about money?

First, you need to know what money is and what it isn't. Money is a measurement of real value. Currency on the other hand is the form that measurement takes place in and a tool of exchange. In today's world we're most familiar with the dollar as currency; however, the widespread and often unchallenged belief is that dollars are money, when in actuality assets are what hold the real value.

ASSETS VS. LIABILITIES

Resource: Read Rich Dad Poor Dad by Robert Kiyosaki

Now that you're starting to see that there is a difference between things that make you seem rich and things that ACTUALLY make you wealthy, let's dive further into it.

The first chapter of *Rich Dad Poor Dad* is titled, "The Rich Don't Work for Money". Kiyosaki goes on to explain that the rich instead have their money do the work of making more money through controlling assets. So, what is an asset? You may be familiar with the term's asset and liability from school, but here we're going to make it very simple and keep it about building wealth.

At their most basic definitions, an asset is something that puts money in your pocket and a liability is something that takes money out of your pocket.

While many people may think an asset is simply something that goes up in value over time or something you can put under the asset column of your financial statement, the value of an asset is determined by the utility it provides. We'll use an example of house.

A 3-bedroom, 2-bathroom house in 1960 might have cost $30K. Today that same 3/2 house probably costs about $300K. What changed? It still only sleeps 3 people and still only has 2 bathrooms. It didn't grow in size.

It still provides the same utility as it did 60 years ago. What changed was the dollar. You now have less purchasing power with your dollars. So, which would you rather have more of - houses that hold their value or dollars that lose their value?

Now let's say you used that house as a rental property to produce income for you. Because it provides real utility, people will pay money for that utility. Instead of buying the house, paying the property expenses and waiting for the value to go up in relation to dollars (which, remember, happen to be falling in real value), you've turned it into a cash-flowing asset that pays an income every month.

What about liabilities?

Liabilities take money out of your pocket. They are costs with no monetary return.

A basic example of this would be a car. The minute you drive a car off the lot it starts to lose its value in terms of dollars.

Furthermore, there are expenses associated with driving and maintaining the car. Could a car become an asset? Absolutely. Take the same car you just bought, rent it out for other people to drive when they're in town, work out a deal with an advertising company so you get paid when you drive.

Essentially, once the car starts to produce cash flow greater than the expenses of the car, you have an asset.

Focus on acquiring assets. If you must take on a liability, make sure you have an income-producing asset to at least cover the expense. This is how you will arrive at financial freedom. It's when the assets you control provide *passive* income equal or greater than your *expenses*.

IMPORTANT HISTORY OF MONEY AND BANKING

*Excerpt from *Real Asset Investing* by Russell Gray

Understanding how money as we know it today came to be, who controls the price of it, where it flows and laws that shape how you interact with it is imperative if you want to master money instead of having it enslave you. I have yet to find a simpler explanation of how our monetary system is as it relates to you than the *Real Asset Investing Report by Russell Gray of the Real Estate Guys.* So instead of me re-inventing the wheel, I'm going to leverage the work of my greatest mentor and re-share his words here to catch you up on how we got to where we're at with money.

I am of the belief that the Fed is the most powerful yet most misunderstood entity on earth. It controls the value of the world's reserve currency, the U.S. dollar. And the U.S. dollar affects every economy and virtually every human being on earth (except maybe the pygmies in some African jungles).

We're talking interest rates, loan availability, the cost of goods and services, and the values of our stocks, bonds, mutual funds, real estate and precious metals. The Fed operates in the shadows, yet their activities permeate every facet of our lives.

Here's a synopsis of how it happened:

In 1913, bankers and politicians conspired... oops... "worked together" to pass The Federal Reserve Act. On the heels of the 16th Amendment, this gave the United States the income tax and the IRS. Great. Prior to that, people were free to keep the fruits of their labors. The government was smaller and more affordable, and was funded largely through foreign trade tariffs and excise taxes.

The purported purpose of all this legislation was to protect the economy from terrible economic events like the Crash of 1907 (never let a good crisis go to waste).

How? By providing emergency liquidity to banks. If you've ever seen the movie *Mary Poppins*, set in England in 1910, then you know how scared bankers are of "runs" (people all wanting their money out at the same time).

Of course, only a few years after the Fed was created, excess liquidity (too much money and credit in the financial system) fueled the wild speculation of the 1920's which culminated in the Great Depression. Oh well. It was a nice idea.

But rather than fix the real problem, Franklin Roosevelt's solution called "The Raw New Deal" included the confiscation of all privately-owned gold. The premise was that "evil hoarders" (a.k.a. savers) were responsible for the crash. If only those pesky savers would actually spend money, then the economy could be stimulated.

Yes, Lord Keynes was in his prime back in those days. This whole scenario began the outright assault on the American virtue of thrift and savings.

HAVE I GOT A DEAL FOR YOU

To be fair, Uncle Sam didn't actually *confiscate* the citizens' gold. He just forced them to sell it to him for $20.67 per ounce. Of course, as soon as Uncle Sam had it all, he re-priced the gold at $35 an ounce. Great deal for Uncle Sam. Not so good for U.S. citizens.

Why there wasn't a revolt right there, I'll never understand. I guess people valued "safety" over freedom. Oops.

"He who sacrifices freedom for security deserves neither."
– Benjamin Franklin

By 1944, between the confiscation of private wealth (the aforementioned gold purchased at a discount) and the profits from financing a couple of world wars and the resulting reparations, Uncle Sam was the proud owner of about 80% of the world's entire gold stock. And back then, gold and money were one and the same. Gold hadn't yet been relegated to the status of "barbarous relic".

Uncle Sam had some big clout. In 1944 he went to a place called Bretton Woods and cut a deal with the rest of the world. Instead of settling international debts with gold, Uncle Sam said, "Just use dollars. They're lighter, easier to count, and you can always turn them into Uncle Sam for real gold. Trust me."

So, the world looked at Uncle Sam's pile of gold, powerful economy and big army and said, "Okay."

For the next 20 years, America boomed. We invented stuff. We built stuff. Smart people came from all over the world to enjoy freedom, opportunity and take their shot at the American Dream. Sure, we started having some cultural issues, but by today's standards, it was Pleasantville.

STEP RIGHT UP AND GET SOME FREE STUFF

And while America got rich, politicians got lazy. They found it was easier to buy votes than to earn them. Just promise people a piece of American prosperity whether they earned it or not and you get all kinds of votes. It's the flaw of democracy when not chained by rule of law. That's why our democratic republic came up with a Constitution and Bill of Rights.

When a person's private property isn't protected by law, then a majority vote can take it. Usually this is done under the cover of some noble cause – children, education, national defense, or helping the poor. Pick one.

Americans are good people and when you tug at their heartstrings because they open their wallets.

The problem is that when you're busy being prosperous and the camel sticks its nose under the tent to nibble from your plate, unless you're intensely principled (like the Founders, who rebelled over what today would be considered a virtually insignificant tax), then you will let it slide.

One day you wake up and the principle is all but forgotten, and private property can be taken and redistributed through a myriad of arcane laws. It didn't happen overnight, of course. It was a series of incremental incursions.

The Federal Reserve Act in 1913 was a big grab. So was the New Deal, the Great Society, the War on Terror, and now the Affordable Care Act. Along the way, there were lots of little ones but they all have their roots in money.

In the mid 60's, Uncle Sam was still thinking he was rich. He created MASSIVE spending programs (Johnson's "Guns and Butter" programs), which outstripped American productivity. Just like when you spend more than you earn, you run... bleed... hemorrhage... red ink.

Thus, the Fed was printing dollars like... well, like dollars... and the world is flooded with them. Back then, you could turn your dollars in for gold unless you were an American citizen, in which case it was still illegal. Go figure.

Side note: Thanks in large part to the courage of one noble patriot named James Blanchard, President Ford finally lifted the ban on private gold ownership in America in 1974. It just proves one guy or gal with a spine can make a difference.

Meanwhile, Uncle Sam's international trading partners started showing up at the "gold window" redeeming their paper dollars for the real thing (gold). And guess what? Uncle Sam starts running out of gold.

On August 15th, 1971, Richard Nixon, by Presidential decree, closed the gold window "temporarily" (we're still waiting...), effectively disconnecting the dollar from gold. His justification? Borrowing from FDR's playbook, he blamed a nameless, faceless villain. FDR blamed "hoarders".

Nixon blamed "speculators". The irony is that unfettering the dollar from gold opened up speculation in financial markets, the likes of which had never been seen.

Also (and the main motivation), with the dollar now effectively disconnected from gold, the Fed was free to fund as much government largesse as it wanted. Who needs a balanced budget when you can just print all the money you want?

No surprise... government debt skyrocketed. Just look at the chart on the next page. Yikes. That's a lot of red ink!

If you're familiar with all this, then you're tracking just fine. Good job. Please don't get bored and skip ahead. Think of it as a trip down memory lane.

Meanwhile, in keeping with the philosophy of *The Real Estate Guys called* "no investor left behind", I need to cover a few more fundamental points.

First, in financial terms a "note" is an IOU. It's like the promissory note you sign when you get a mortgage or a car loan. It means you, the issuer of the note or "note maker", owes the lender or the "note holder". Make sense?

Let's take a look at a greenback. I chose a twenty-dollar bill because it has a picture of Andrew Jackson. He was the President who successfully dismantled the second attempt at a Central Bank in the United States way back in 1833. It was 80 years before it was resurrected in the form of *The Creature from Jekyll Island* (sorry...that line was too good to pass up), which is the Federal Reserve Bank that we now have.

By the way, *The Creature from Jekyll Island* is the name of a book on this very topic.

Notice that the note is called a Federal Reserve *Note* (FRN). That means you are the note holder (the person owed). And the Fed is the note maker – the one who owes.

The problem is that since 1971, you can't turn it in for gold anymore. So, what is it good for? Paying taxes and that's it. Because other people need dollars to pay their taxes too, they will trade your goods and services for your FRNs. This is why having an income tax is important. It creates a demand for these otherwise useless pieces of paper.

The irony is that the Federal government doesn't need taxes to pay its bills. And they know it.

TRUE CONFESSIONS
OF A MAD BANKER

In fact, back in January 1946, then Chairman of the Federal Reserve Bank of New York, Beardsley Ruml, gave a speech before the American Bar Association. What he admitted publicly is shocking.

*"**The necessity for a government to tax in order to maintain both its independence and its solvency** is true for state and local governments, but it **is not true for national government**."* [Emphasis mine]

Why? Because state and local governments don't have a printing press. They can't just create money to fund profligate spending so they go broke. Just ask the cites of Stockton, California; Vallejo, California; and Detroit, Michigan.

But it gets better...

"Two changes of the greatest consequence have occurred in the last twenty-five years, which have substantially altered the position of the national state with respect to the financing of its current requirements.

The first of these changes is the gaining of vast new experience in the management of central banks.

The second change is the elimination, for domestic purposes, of the convertibility of the currency into gold."

Remember, this was back in 1946. Foreigners could still turn dollars into gold.

Of course, since Nixon closed the gold window in 1971, today NO ONE can go to the Fed to convert paper into metal. Once again, thanks to James Blanchard and President Ford, at least you can convert paper to metal in the open market. Which means Uncle Sam gets to keep all his gold. Clever.

TAX MATTERS

The next question is why tax if the government doesn't need the money? After all, it only makes the voters mad.

Basically, Ruml said the purpose of taxes is to *control businesses and effect social control*. Really. Those are his exact words. This is why I don't think the system will change anytime soon. Those in power hate to give it up.

I know. It sounds like conspiracy theory.

You don't have to trust me on this. You can read it yourself from the source document, which is a scanned image of the original publication, *American Affairs, January 1946, Volume VIII, No. 1*. I'll even make it easy for you. Just send an email to ruml@realestateguysradio.com and I'll send it you.

Again, I'm not trying to be political. I'm just explaining how the system works, why it's unlikely to change, how it affects you, and (if you're patient...) what you can do to protect and grow your wealth inside of a system that is truly counter-intuitive.

BECAUSE I SAID SO

Now back to our perusal of the greenback...

Do you see how the FRN says "This note is legal tender for all debts public and private"?

In fact, this decree (called a legal tender law) or "fiat" (why people call unbacked currency "fiat currency") is what gives a piece of paper value. Otherwise, it's not really much good for anything. It has no intrinsic value like a commodity such as gold, silver, oil, etc. The only reason people accept it is because they are compelled to. And because they trust the next person will accept it, too.

When that trust starts to fade, people will look for alternatives. Like Bitcoin.

Again, sorry if this is too basic. But without this fundamental understanding, the rest of this pieces of the puzzle won't make as much sense.

TAKE THESE... I INSIST

The Fed gets to print as many of these notes as they want (paper or electronic), which are basically IOU's that the Fed never has to repay in real money (gold).

And through legal tender laws, all U.S. citizens are forced to "buy" dollars (by trading their labor and productivity to collect FRNs to pay taxes).

And through the Bretton Woods deal, all foreign countries have to buy dollars to settle their international trade.

That's a lot of "have to" demand for U.S. dollars. In a free market, demand is usually the result of "want to" because the item being offered rises to the top of the competition. For decades the U.S. dollar has really not had any competition.

Can you imagine if YOU were permitted to sit down and write, print or otherwise fabricate, as many IOU's as you could create, knowing that you could go out into the market and use them to buy real goods, services and commodities? Absent any moral hindrance, how many would YOU print? Exactly. A gazillion.

Sure, if you went on a bender and got carried away, you might promise to taper. All addicts promise to stop. But they can't. Why would you want to stop? Just slow down a little and hope no one cares enough to do anything about it.

Make sense?

If this info is still unclear, it is a complex topic and why I urge you to study it on your own. A great place to start would be by reading the entire report.

So where are we now? Well, the Fed is still in place and continues to act as you just read. The exciting news is that we are on the forefront of a changing monetary system – we're seeing this in the rise of crypto currency as way for people to have more control of their money. And with dramatic change comes dramatic opportunities.

In continuing with the financial knowledge, you need to have so YOU too can be in control of your financial well-being, let's discuss the different types of income and the different ways to generate money.

TYPES OF INCOME

When condensed down, there really are only three types of income – earned, passive and portfolio.

Earned income is money you generate from exchanging your time and/or effort for dollars. This generally comes in the form of a job. This is not the best path for quickly building wealth and certainly not the best route for gaining freedom.

Passive income is generated from things like investments, rental income, royalties, etc. This type of income is passively flowing in, meaning you are not directly exchanging your time and effort for the money. Another term for passive income is cash flow.

Portfolio income is produced and also passive; the distinction is in the asset. Portfolio income would come from paper assets such as stocks, bonds, and notes.

Now that you know the different types of income, next you'll learn the different capacities those incomes are made.

ESBI

While there are literally thousands upon thousands of ways to actually go about making money, there are four categories all those ways fit into. This concept of ESBI is known as the Cashflow Quadrant from Robert Kiyosaki. He has a book which dives deep into this idea called *The Cashflow Quadrant*, which I highly recommend you study.

What does ESBI mean?

It is an acronym for Employee, Self-Employed, Business Owner and Investor. The important thing to understand, in addition to what the different ways entail in terms of activity, is how the income is taxed.

Employee – Employees make earned income. They exchange their precious time and energy for a paycheck from a boss. These are some of the hardest working people. Unfortunately, in a rigged monetary system; hard work doesn't get them ahead. This is largely in part to the fact that Employee income is taxed almost the highest – 30%. On top of that, the steep tax on your income is taken out BEFORE you get your paycheck. Even if you wanted to invest your money into better vehicles, you don't even get a chance to do so.

A huge chunk is taken before you see it. And the more you work and the more you earn here, the more they take. This is why being an employee puts you at a huge disadvantage in the real world.

Self-Employed – This is where most entrepreneurs end up stuck. The self-employed person doesn't have a job - they own their job. Meaning, although they may have a business, if they don't show up to operate the business, the business stops producing income. Thus, they are like employees in that they are still trading their time and energy for income. Hopefully, the business is at least something they love devoting their time to. Also, self-employed people are taxed the highest and in the same way employees are – BEFORE they get paid. So again, while it may seem you have more control of your lifestyle and income, you're still fighting a huge uphill battle to succeed here.

Business Owner – This where the tables turn. Business owners build businesses run by systems and processes that don't require them being IN the business in order for it to produce income and continue to grow. Jobs are good for the economy, so the government encourages business owners by not taking them in the same way as E's and S's. Instead of the income being taxed before you get paid, the money flows directly to you FIRST. This gives much more control over where and how your money is allocated. Sure, you still have to pay taxes, but it is significantly less and at the end of the day, the rules of money were written by the rich, FOR the rich. So, if one is to take the time be financially educated, they will easily be able to find ways within the tax code to decrease the amount of tax they pay.

Investor – These are the people who use their money, or even better, other people's money (OPM) to make more money. This category is also taxed the least. This is where you want be.

In a conversation with Robert Kiyosaki, I asked him, "What is the biggest difference between the rich and the poor?" He answered, "The biggest difference is the way they THINK about money and HOW they handle their fear." While the technicalities of the ways to make money is important to understand, it is far more important that you understand and begin thinking the way the rich do. Just because you are currently an employee or self-employed, it doesn't mean you have to think like one. Begin thinking like a Business Owner and Investor. Approach money like they would and watch how your results start to dramatically change.

The last concept I'll introduce to you here is around the idea of debt.

GOOD DEBT VS. BAD DEBT

When most people hear the word 'debt', they cringe with a bad feeling. Understandably so, because the only 'debt' they've dealt with has probably been overwhelming credit card payments, gargantuan student loans or lingering medical bills. Indeed, these are all bad 'debts. However, debt isn't always bad. Debt can be a powerful tool in the game of money. Kiyosaki says, "Debt is like a handgun, it can be used to harm you or it can be used to protect you." Knowing how to use the gun will determine if it hurts you or helps you. In the same way, knowing how to use debt – which comes from financial education – will determine whether you are consumed by it or are empowered by it.

To understand how good debt works, we'll use an example of two people. Each person is buying a house.

Let's say you want to start investing and now that you understand that real estate is one of the best REAL assets there is, you find a house you want to buy.

Let's say the house costs $100,000. Person A, without financial education who thinks debt is bad, might say, well I don't want to take on any new debt. Since I don't have $100,000, I can't buy this house – and he might miss out on a great opportunity.

Or let's say he has the $100,000 and because he thinks all debt is bad, he might want to buy the house paid in full. That's fine but again, he is limiting the return on the investment by approaching it this way.

Person B with financial education and understanding that debt can be a powerful tool might approach it in a different way. Although he might only have $20,000 to buy the house, he uses the $20,000 as a down payment and gets a loan for the remaining $80,000. He now controls the property, gets a tenant in it, and receives rental income.

When Person A buys the house for $100,000 out of pocket and Person B buys the house with only $20,000 out of pocket, both own the house. However, the amount invested by Person B is significantly less. Someone might look at Person B and say, well they're $80,000 in debt. While this is true, it is good debt because with $20,000 he is controlling a $100,000 asset that someone else (the renter) is paying off PLUS gaining a little extra in the form of rent.

If both had the full $100,000 to start, by taking Person B's approach, instead of just controlling one $100,000 property, he can do the same thing with four more houses and control a half-million dollars' worth of real assets that puts money in the pocket every month. Person A would have to continue to work hard and save up enough money to do it again.

This book is about accelerating your success. As far as building real wealth and financial freedom fast, which path makes more sense?

Good debt allows you to control more with less and build passive income while doing so. Bad debt ties up your money, costs you money and limits your opportunities. The idea to grasp is that debt can be used as leverage.

It is possible to become overleveraged to the point where you can't keep up with the debt service. However, when you master financial modeling and continue your real estate investing education, you'll be able to make sound decisions and set up a structure that protects you.

My hope is that now you're starting to look at money a little differently because, remember, that's the biggest difference between the rich and the poor. The concepts we covered here are the tip of the iceberg and if you want to truly get ahead in the real world, it's imperative you have a solid financial education.

Before you attack the world, start business and begin designing your ideal lifestyle begin practicing interacting with money the way the rich do.

REAL WORLD ACTIONS:

Read: *The Creature From Jekyll Island*
           by G. Edward Griffin
Attend: Freedom Fest

           Look for ways to add value to others.

CHAPTER 6.
STEP 5 – DESIGN YOUR LIFESTYLE

"If you don't design your own life plan, chances are you'll fall into someone else's plan, and guess what they have planned for you? Not much."
– Jim Rohn

In 1990, boxer James 'Buster' Douglas fought Iron Mike Tyson for the Heavyweight Championship of the world. In spite of Douglas losing his mom just two days before the fight, he got in the ring anyway.

As the fight went on, it was clear Tyson was the champion for a reason. He punished Douglas and nearly ended the fight when he landed a brutal right hook that dropped Douglas. Buster was lying on the canvas with the ref standing over him counting 7….8….9…ding-ding-ding, saved by the bell.

Everyone watching thought for sure Tyson would finish Douglas in the next round. Sure enough, Tyson came out and began to land punches at will. Then something in Douglas changed while he was up against the ropes and taking a beating, Buster Douglas started swinging back. The world watched in astonishment as the fight quickly turned around. Everyone was left in shock when Buster Douglas knocked Mike Tyson out.

After the fight the newscasters asked Douglas, what happened?

He told them what was going through his mind during the fight. He told them how much pain he was in, how he didn't want get up off the canvas and that he wanted to quit but he couldn't. He was sitting in his corner right before that last round, and he recalls that he remembered 'why'—why he got in the ring with Mike Tyson just two days after his mom died. It's what he had to do.

He remembered that his mom told him long before the fight was even scheduled that soon he would beat Mike Tyson and become heavyweight champion of the world. This was his one shot. His opportunity to fulfill what his mom had told him. His opportunity to be the best.

The 'why' Douglas had was stronger than anything that could happen to him. Any hit he was going to wear he could wear because of his 'why'. Even if he got knocked down, he was going to continue to fight. His 'why' was stronger than all the reasons he had to quit.

You need to discover your 'why'. Writing down goals is great and there is certainly power in doing so, but life will knock you down and every time it does doubt will come in and you'll think "Maybe these goals aren't for me… maybe my goals are unrealistic… maybe I should find any easier path." If your goals aren't rooted in a stronger purpose, when life knocks you down, instead of having the strength to get up and fight back like Buster Douglas did, you'll give into those thoughts and into the pain and quit. In your most trying times, it will be your 'why' that keeps you fighting.

Many people drift through life never achieving the outcomes they want, only to end up with regret. A major reason this happens is because they don't take enough time to develop a big enough 'why' for their lives. They don't allow themselves to have the experiences that give them clarity. They get caught up in the urgencies of life and trap themselves in commitments that don't serve their bigger purpose, all because they did what they were told.

They lived their lives on someone else's terms, never giving themselves the opportunity to discover what it is they truly want out of life. I encourage you to take the time to uncover what it is you want your life to look like. Develop a why. It must be bigger than money, bigger than serving the ego, and bigger than the sacrifices you'll have to make.

"But, Sean, I don't know my 'why'. I have no idea what my greater purpose is…"

I completely understand. It took me a whole bunch of life experiences and making several U-turns on my life path to uncover my purpose.

Nonetheless, if you are struggling to figure out what your purpose is and aren't able to answer that question clearly, this means it is time to take action. Your 'why' will get clearer through experiences. Finding your purpose can seem difficult. And it is, but simply follow your passions, because your passions will eventually lead you to your purpose. It's going to narrow down and it's going to get clearer but the things you are passionate about will point you in the direction of the value you want to add.

For example, I was passionate about football. And then I went through a process of asking myself several revealing questions – mostly the question 'why?' over and over again until I got to the root of why I loved football so much.

What I found out was that the actual game of football wasn't the thing that truly fulfilled me. What I was passionate about was inside of football—the competition and the camaraderie. Then I went down further and said, "What about that do I like?" I like being able to help out the younger guy. What I really like is coaching and leading people who trust me – to success.

I eventually arrived at a point of clarity in THE thing that really fulfilled me - my 'why' moving forward. I would have never been able to identify it without going through that questioning process and having the experience of being immersed in an environment that I enjoyed for eighteen years.

Now, it manifests in what I am doing. I get to teach. I get to coach and inspire other people, and that's the aspect of football that I loved. I loved inspiring my teammates—I loved leading my teammates. It wasn't necessarily football. It was those core values. I was simply following my passion of football, and it led me to my purpose of coaching, inspiring and empowering—teaching others. If you follow your passions, your purpose will eventually come out, but you must take action.

Maybe you're at a point where you're not even sure what you're really passionate about. You might be thinking, I don't have something I'm super excited about like you had with football. What then?

Answer the following question. Imagine I write you a check for $100,000 today. When you wake up tomorrow, you get a new check for another $100K, and the next day and the next. Money is no longer an issue for you. How would you spend your time? What would you do on a day-to-day basis? What is going to make you want to jump out of bed in the morning that you want to start doing even though you don't need the money?

What came to mind? Travel? Spend time with family? Help others? Finally launch that passion project you've had in mind?

Whatever it looks like, keep asking yourself why. "Why this or why that... well, why is that? What about that do I like so much? And so, on and so on until you get to the deepest reason of why you want what you say you want. Once you have the why in mind, once you have the end in mind, the steps to get there will become obvious.

When you're clear on your why and your vision, and you know the actions you need to take to fulfill it, that is the point where you're able to sprint in a confident direction. It's also the point where you'll feel retired, where work and pleasure will become indistinguishable.

Nobody can do this for you, nor would you want him or her to because no one cares about what you want as much as you do. When it comes to designing your life, don't settle. Don't let someone else be in control of your precious and irreplaceable time. A job often robs you of your freedom, creativity and choice. Thankfully, there are so many ways to make money outside of a job. It comes down to you taking the time to think it through, find your why, and get the end in mind and design of your own life.

If you don't design your own life plans, chances are you'll fall into someone else's. And guess what they have planned for you—not much.

Still feel unclear? Take action. Action leads to clarity. Clarity leads to decisiveness. Decisiveness leads to more results, and more results leads to greater success.

Don't get me wrong; even when you have a clear vision there will still be times when you feel unsure or scared. I remember writing in my journal at a time when I felt this, here's what I wrote:

"I am feeling stuck and overwhelmed. I am starting to realize how much work it actually is to build what I want to build. It's almost as if I am looking for a good excuse to quit.

Why is that? How do I get past that? This isn't something I want to admit, much less, talk with a mentor about. It's embarrassing."

I was getting overwhelmed and fearful of how much work I actually had to put in and whether I was truly headed in the right direction. That's what I was feeling. And I wrote, "I feel like I am almost looking for a good excuse, at this point, to quit." I was so overwhelmed and scared that I was looking for a good excuse to quit.

But I didn't, because right at my desk, I had my 'why' written out in front of me.

Seeing your why written out and reading it when you start to doubt will be a great tool to inspire you to continue...just like it worked for Buster Douglas.

When you're clear on the vision of your life and internalized your 'why', that is when you can begin setting your goals to bring it reality. Setting these goals is an entire process in itself. And it's crucial to understand the different types of goals and what is in your control and what isn't.

There are two types of goals – performance goals and outcome goals. You can't control the outcome, but you most certainly are in control of your performance. Losing 30 pounds would be an outcome goal. Drinking 20 glasses of water a day, running 2 miles everyday, or eating an apple a day would be examples of performance goals. The 30 lbs. coming off your body frame is a result of your performance.

Performance goals are micro steps that you CAN do. They are short-term milestones to keep you going in the right direction. Outcome goals are longer term and are the results of your performance.

The simple fact that life throws you curve balls and gives you unexpected circumstances out of your control is why you can't control outcome goals. It's dangerous to think you can control outcomes and even more dangerous to attach your success to a destination.

Goals are directions, not destinations.

When you reach a goal, what do you do? You set a new goal. It's like an infinite line of dots that you're connecting. If each dot is a goal along your path, then there's no final destination because once you reach the next dot you keep drawing, or once you reach your goal you don't just stop. Life goes on.

When you're attached to the outcome or if you are rigidly set on a particular outcome, you limit it being even better than you'd imagine. You'll be less flexible in your approach and you'll say no to things that might actually be more beneficial. If you measure success as progress, then even if you don't get your initially intended outcome, you're successful because you've progressed.

Entrepreneurship is less about knowing the ins-and-outs of business and more about managing your emotions and self-worth. Sadly, when people attach to a desired outcome, they often tie up their identity in whether or not they achieve their goal. They are measuring their success in outcomes that they have little control over. This is why I measure success in progress. It makes it a lot easier NOT to quit when you measure success in progress. Most entrepreneurs fail because they don't have an extremely clear vision, financial education or great sales skills. However, many entrepreneurs quit because they feel like failures when they aren't seeing the results they wanted so badly. They give up because in their mind they aren't succeeding since they're measuring success as a destination.

How do you make sure you're staying on track and progressing along your goals?

One of the best ways is to write your goals down and keep them in places where you'll constantly view them. Time blocking is another major key.

Set appointments with yourself and stick to them as if it was someone you greatly respect. If you don't take yourself seriously why would someone else?

If you feel stuck or lost, make a list of things you can do to progress.

For me, having a list of the things I am going to accomplish in the day is huge. It's written in my own handwriting, placed where I can see it—so, when I wake up, I don't feel lost. If I am confused, I can just look down and say, "Okay, these are the things I said I was going to do today." And always at the top of the list is the one thing I can do. That item is the thing that when I do it, everything else becomes easier and necessary.

One of the most important elements of goal setting is accountability. This is where surrounding yourself with the right people is absolutely paramount.

When you write down goals and you make a big commitment to something, you are in that state of high emotion. Follow through comes when you are committed. Commitment is staying true to what you said you would do long after the feelings at the time you said it are gone. A way to help with that commitment is to set up the accountability and social support. Surround yourself with people who have similar goals; even if they just have goals in general, and hold each other accountable.

The difference between 'good' and 'great' is really not that big. The difference between the good college football players and the great college football players—the good NFL players and the great NFL players is not a big difference. But at the same time, it makes all the difference.

Take a 40-yard dash for example. The difference between 4.3 seconds and 4.5 seconds is a very small amount, but it's a huge in terms of value and the effort it took the athlete to get to a 4.3. It's the sum total of the little things compounding over time. It's the accumulation of the little efforts every single day.

If you feel like you can't make strides, just do the little things consistently. Focus on the things you can do and be consistent with them.

For example, take two people both with the same physical shape. One person eats vegetables every day and one other eats a donut every day. In a day, you are not going to really tell the difference. A week later, you are still not really going to be able to tell the difference. A month later, maybe still there's no visible difference.

But six months down the road, you will see effects of what they've been eating. Five years down the road, there will be a dramatic difference.

We often look at where people are at in life and think that it just happened for them overnight. Giving up on your goals and dreams because of the time it takes to reach them is ridiculous. The time is going to pass anyway. Understand that success is a lifestyle and success is progress. It's not a destination. When you internalize this, it makes doing those little things consistently every day much easier.

Are there going to be times when you don't follow through? Will there be times when you get off track? Of course, and it comes in the form of resistance.

In one of my favorite books by Stephen Presfield called *Turning Pro*, he talks about this concept in great detail, but here are some of the way's resistance might show up in your life...

1. Television
2. Surfing the Internet watching music videos and celebrity gossip
3. Scrolling through Instagram over and over again
4. Hitting every happy hour and the bars on the weekend

It's the things we do to avoid doing what we really know we should be doing. And sometimes it's not always that obvious.

Many times, people live, as Stephen Presfield calls, 'shadow careers'. Some people just spend excessive amounts of time in the gym exercising to avoid taking the risk of pursuing their truest and best life. They feel like they are productive and they feel like they are doing something good, but deep down it's not what they know that they want out of life.

If you feel like you can't get started building your dreams because you think you don't know the right people, you don't have enough money, or you have too much debt or not enough time, there is something you can do. Just start where you're at with you what you have.

And like Tony Robbins says, you don't lack resources – you lack resourcefulness. It's cliché but true, if there is a will – there is a way.

It is heartbreaking to see people forego their passions and dreams because of their own limiting beliefs. What's even more heartbreaking is when it's your family and friends. That's why I am so passionate about young people. I narrowly avoided the trap earlier than most. Yet I could have easily made the decision to say, "Sure, this looks like a good marketing company. I'll take a job with them."

Then the next thing you know, I've racked up debt in the form of liabilities because I got used to the paychecks coming in. Next the urgencies of the career take over and I'm ten years down the road thinking it's too late now to chase my dreams.

I feel fortunate I had people ask me great questions that changed some paradigms for me. But that one small decision would have had a ripple effect on the direction of my life.

We only get one life and it's short. How do you really want to be living your life?

Only you can answer that and only you should answer that. The cool thing about having dreams and what you believe is that dreams don't require anyone else except you to believe in them. If you have a dream or goal and you believe in it, don't let anyone tell you, 'You can't achieve it" or "Your dream isn't realistic." Define your vision. Live each day and take every action with purpose and direction towards that.

You must be able to design and see the big picture, and then be able to put your head down and work like crazy to get there. The challenge is not getting lost in the weeds.

Imagine swimming in salt water towards an object. You can't swim with your eyes open because it's too painful and distracting. But you can't hold your head above water and swim either –because then you are not moving fast enough. So, you have to take a minute above the water to see where that object is, then put your head down and close your eyes and swim as hard as you can in that direction. To keep yourself from going off-course, you have to stop every now and again, get the object in sight, make sure you are heading in the right direction, and then put your head down and swim again.

You can't change how far and where the object is, but you can control how you swim. And you do that by focusing on what you can do right now, and doing it.

When you have a vision you are committed to, it becomes a lifestyle and work suddenly becomes pleasure. It's not all sunshine and rainbows. It takes hard work and discipline. If you are willing to invest a few years of your life like most people won't, you can spend the rest of your life like most people can't.

And don't worry. Sometimes feeling lost is a part of the journey. We all experience it. It is, without a doubt, a process. Sometimes, it's hard to tell if you are just in a long, deep, dark valley or you have gone completely off course.

Sometimes it feels like you put in a tremendous amount of effort and you don't seem to get anywhere. Some days, the boulder you are pushing is rolling smoothly uphill.

And other days, it takes everything in you just to keep the boulder from rolling backwards and crushing you. When you experience this, remember these three things: One, this too shall pass. No valley lasts forever so have patience.

Two, remember why you started. What is the mission and vision? And is what I am doing moving me closer or farther away from it? And three, keep pushing. Don't let up. Don't give up. Some progress is better than no progress. Hard work pays off.

If you ever feel stuck or not sure what to do to make progress, grab a book and start reading. It might not seem like a huge step towards your goals, but at least, you are taking action. And as we know, action brings clarity. Remember you are only one great idea—one great relationship away from explosion in your life or career. You never know where that idea is going to come from. So, give yourself as many opportunities to have great ideas as possible. Fill your mind with the right stuff and put yourself in the right environments.

There are going to be a lot of seemingly dead ends that you travel. It's fine. You are gaining the feedback necessary to make the change in your direction. You are getting experiences and you are learning things about yourself—about what you like and what you don't like – how you like spending your time and how you don't— and getting more and more clarity with those actions.

Pursue something. For example, I thought I wanted to do a podcast, so I started pursuing podcasting. I took action. I went to a podcast conference and I started doing courses, investing time, money and effort into learning and starting that venture. Then I got to a point where I really understood what it took to produce a truly successful podcast. And I said, "Actually, this is not how I want to spend my time."

There were several other paths I started to go, only to turn around and say, "No, that's not what I want to do." But that's not a failure. If I didn't do those things, I wouldn't have known if I wanted to do those things or not. I got feedback and more clarity, but I never stopped taking action.

Lastly, we keep talking about clarity and how important gaining clarity is. Clarity isn't something that just takes a moment to think up. It's not what you get from one workshop or one podcast or one idea. Clarity is something that develops over time, through experience.

Walk confidently in the direction of your goals. Fail fast, fail forward and fail frequently. Don't view failure as failure but only as an opportunity to grow and improve. Failure isn't a dead end. It's the exact opposite. It means you had the courage to go for it and ultimately progress. Failure is not the antithesis of success. Failure is success because success is progress.

In the next chapter, we'll explain the one skill you need to master in order to make your vision a reality.

REAL WORLD ACTIONS:

Read: *Life on Purpose* by Victor J. Strecher
Attend: Create Your Future with Robert Helms

              Look for ways to add value to others.

CHAPTER 7.
STEP 6 – MASTER THE ONE SKILL YOU NEED

"Great sales isn't a signed contract...it's how people feel about you when they leave."
- Sean D. Gray

Imagine being able to get into a conversation with any caliber or profile of person and then walking away from that interaction with the other person feeling ecstatic about meeting you PLUS you get what you want? Just think what it would be like to go into any situation and know you can get people to not just like you, but be excited to help you.

Now imagine you never learned how to do that and struggle to get your way. You struggle to get into relationships with mentors, potential clients, and ultimately struggle to make money? How would that feel? What would that life be like?

Well, there is good news right here on the horizon. This skill is very much learnable. And the skill is sales. If you can communicate, you can be trained to sell effectively.

Now before you jump to the thought that "I'm not a salesperson!" and "Sales isn't for me!" or "I'm an introvert so I won't be good at it," think about this because you just might be a better salesperson than you think.

We are all constantly selling. Whether we're selling ourselves to a possible partner, or getting someone to see things from our perspective, or an idea, product or service.

If you've ever had someone agree to go on a date with you, that's sales. If you've ever won a debate, that's sales. If you've ever had a group agree on which restaurant to go to, you made a sale.

Sales is NOT about being pushy or manipulating people into buying things they don't really want or need. Master salesmanship is the art of diagnosing a problem, recommending a solution, and persuading people to move forward in their own best interest. It's about identifying problems, uncovering people's needs, wants, goals and desires and then offering solutions and gaining agreement to implement those solutions. It's about how people feel about you after interacting with you.

If you have the ability to sell, you have the ability to make money whenever you need to, get into any relationship you want to, and even get people to work for you for free.

The skill of sales is THE skill that allows you to get your way in business and life.

Like me, you've likely had several experiences with bad sales people. Maybe it was when you were buying a new car or shopping around for a new place to live. It almost makes you feel gross on the inside. The person probably didn't really listen to you, talked a lot about how much of a great deal he can get you, and of course told you that you can trust him.

Or maybe it was an old friend from high school who hits you up out of the blue to recruit you to his or her MLM. The first thing he says is something like, "I want to talk to you about a cool opportunity" without even asking how you're doing or seeing if he can help you somehow before he asks you for something. He starts with the "I want" perspective from the get go. The interaction is already about what he wants and what he can get.

That's bad sales. Untrained salespeople have given the term 'sales' a bad connotation. But don't let those experiences make you believe that sales talk is some evil trick only used by greedy people. Don't let their bad behavior stop you from studying and mastering it for yourself.

Sales is literally in everything. Right now, as you are reading this book, I am selling you on the idea of going through this process. I'm selling you on taking action and investing in yourself. I have to sell you every chapter that the next chapter is going to be worth reading. So, it goes so much beyond a transaction. It's communication.

If your only goal is to get the contract signed and paid as opposed to making a win-win-win scenario, you will soon be exposed. Time will either promote or expose you. Every conversation and every sale is building up your reputation. How are you leaving people feeling about you?

The difference between great salespeople and bad salespeople comes down to whether they have a hunter or farmer mentality. The hunter mentality is just going for the throat. Do what you have to do to get the sales or get their money. Once you get their money, forget them. Get onto the next one.

Every single day, the lion wakes up and goes out for the kill. That literally puts you on the perpetual cycle of, every single day, you have to do the same thing.

The bigger picture here—not just in terms of one-on-one selling, but of also building your business is to do it in a way that doesn't trap you in owning a job.

You are going to be exchanging your time and effort for dollars and have to do that every single day.

The flipside is the farmer mentality—the idea of planting a seed, nurturing it, watering it, taking care of it and watching it grow. And if you do it right, in due time, it will bear fruits. And then, those fruits, their seeds aka referrals, they can plant more seeds. And it grows on itself.

The hunter has to go out and go for the throat every single day, where the farmer spends planting seeds and having patience. They nurture and water the seeds, and then they reap the fruits of their labor in the future. Which will you be?

Before we go on to how good sales works, I want to remind you this is a guide to get you started in the right direction of mastering sales. You must continue to study, practice and sharpen your skills. Everything you read here was taught to me by my mentors and two of the greatest salespeople I've ever met. The first is legendary sales trainer and author of *Master the Art of Selling* who was a mentor to my dad, who then went and mastered what Tom had taught him and combined it with his own experience, which he has now taught to me. I am a product of my mentors and you will be too.

In fact, mastering this skill will allow you to get into any mentorship you want without paying for it and sometimes without even asking.

How does the sales process work?

First, it is exactly that - a process. It's a fractal process that builds on itself. The key is to know where you're at in the process based on listening to what the other person is saying.

Before we dive into the process, the number one thing to remember if you truly want to be a master salesman is that it's never, ever, ever, ever...never ever, ever about you. Nobody cares about what you want. Everyone wants to know what's in it for them. Like Zig Ziglar famously said, "You can get all you want in life if you just help enough other people get what they want."

The sales process is really simple. I think that a lot of people overcomplicate sales. When you understand how simple the process is and if you are able to identify which part of the process that you are in, in any conversation, it makes it so much easier to communicate and be able to sell.

The sales process is this: Set the table, touch the heart, and engage the mind. Sure, within those, there are different techniques and useful phrases, however in this chapter we'll stick to the process.

So, the first step in the process is what my mentor calls, setting the table.

Setting the table is all about building rapport. People do business with people they know, like and trust. So why you?

Why should they trust you? If they don't know you then they aren't able to feel comfortable with you. Establish common ground; this causes them to feel like they can relate to you, like you're on their side -- which you are.

This is also the step where you build up your own credibility. Be careful not to do this in an arrogant way that says "Hey, look at how great I am." Again, it's never ever ever ever, never ever ever about you. However, you do need them to believe that you are capable of solving their problem. Ideally at this point, you know you can and that's why you're meeting with this person. By this point in time, you also want to be sure you're sitting down with the actual decision maker. Often times there's a spouse, parent, or business partner who has to clear the decision. There is no point on selling someone who can't make the decision to do business with you.

The next step is to touch the person's heart. This is really where the sale happens because people buy emotionally. People buy out of fear or greed. They buy out of pain or pleasure. And all of that is based on emotions. When the heart wants something, it puts an order into the brain's thinking processes and says, "Brain, I need to get this or I need to have this."

Vice versa can also be true. When the heart feels attacked or vulnerable, it orders the brain, *"Protect me. Figure out what to say to protect me."*

The sale really happens in the heart because people buy emotionally. Then they defend it logically.

The way you touch the heart is to uncover what's important to the person.

You have to figure out what their heart tunes or heart strings are playing and how you do that is by asking questions.

There is a huge distinction between great salespeople and lousy salespeople. Great sales people ask great questions. And again, that's why listening is so important. Really, what you are doing is simply asking questions in a sales environment. You are not talking about all the features and benefits and all that stuff your product or service can do. They are smart enough to figure all that stuff out on their own if their heart wants it.

It's actually better when they figure it out on their own because then it's not somebody telling them what to do. They realize it for themselves. Once their heart places the order, the realization is there. Logically, you can see something; everyone has had a situation where they are thinking, "Yeah, makes sense but I just don't have a good feeling about this."

I know we have all heard that from others before, right? "It just doesn't feel right. My gut feeling is telling me no.

I know it makes sense and the numbers work and everything like that, but something isn't right. This is exactly the feeling that holds people back.

In this type of situation, whoever is doing the selling didn't do a good job of uncovering what the issues are. The heart will tell you what their biggest objections are, which really is what their fears are. The heart will also tell you what their greatest desires are and what they really want.

If you can anchor whatever it is that you are selling to how what you have can solve that pain or provide them that pleasure, then that's where the sale is made. Using words like *"Imagine"* or *"Think about what it would be like"* are words that trigger ownership.

It puts them in that feeling that they have it already. If I am selling a product, I might say, *"Imagine having the time and freedom to be able to spend with your family and be able to do things that you want. Imagine how great that would feel."* Use words like 'feel' and get them in the state of owning that.

Touching the heart is all about uncovering their needs, wants, goals and desires. It's about asking questions that reveal what's in their heart.

Then you transition to the last step of the process. However, before you do, you have to make sure you've uncovered every fear and objection they have so that you can overcome it and put them at ease in moving forward.

A great way to do this is by saying, *"So you said you wanted X and Y and the biggest thing you need is Z is that right?"* Assuming you heard them correctly and they agree, the next thing you might ask is, *"So if we can figure out a solution to Z so you can have X and Y, is there any other reason you wouldn't want to move forward with me?"*

By asking this, you're double-checking that you didn't miss any of their objections or fears so you don't go into engaging the mind while they're still hesitant or unsure about what they want.

At this point in the conversation, the person you're talking with should feel like they know you, like you and trust you. They should see you as a credible authority figure. And now that you have tapped into their heart's desires and emotional hot buttons, it's time to engage the mind and show them how the logical steps to get what they said they wanted.

Engaging the mind is the most analytical step as you're explaining the features and more importantly the benefits of whatever it is, you're selling. You are helping them connect the dots from the order their heart placed to defend it logically.

Far too often, people skip right over the touching the heart step. But people buy emotionally and defend it logically.

Poor salespeople go straight into engaging the mind. And when you do that, people feel like they are being sold because they have no emotional investment into the conversation or into the product or the service. Their heart hasn't placed the order yet. Knowing where you are at in any conversation during this process is crucial.

There may be times when you think you've set the table so you start to transition to touching the heart, but then get met with unexpected resistance to going down the path with you. What is usually the case here is that you might not have built enough rapport with the person. Or maybe you haven't established yourself as someone they should listen to.

They might not fully trust you yet. You have to be able to recognize this based off the words they're saying, the hesitation in their voice, and the questions they're asking.

Maybe their questions are focused on you or your company. Well, you haven't done enough table setting yet. Back off from the heart. You don't want to get too intimate too soon.

Come back up to setting the table and get them to know, like, and trust you.

Obviously, the faster you can get them to know, like, and trust you, the better—especially in things like door to door sales or if you have limited time with someone.

Every conversation and every person are different; you have to pay attention to where you are in the process.

You might be moving on to the engaging the mind step to explain the features and the benefits and how the product works, but maybe they aren't emotionally invested yet. They may be kind of quiet or start to hold back and are not as engaged. This tells you didn't go deep enough into the heart. You haven't brought up enough pain or enough pleasure. You have to come back up to the heart. If you are trying to engage the mind or touch the heart but they don't even really know who you are or why they should buy from you or worse yet, they might not even like you, then you are going to blow it.

As you can see, the sales process is not necessarily a linear one, two, three process. Sales aren't a presentation. It's a conversation. Every sales situation is going to be different because everybody thinks different. Dealing with a really analytical person like an engineer means you are going to spend a lot more time setting the table and engaging the mind because that's the way they think. If you are talking with a person who is a real skeptic and the first thing is no to everything, you are going to spend a lot more time setting the table. But really, the art of selling is asking great questions.

Just because you make sense in your sales pitch and got the person to feel like they can trust you doesn't mean it's going to be an easy 'yes' from them. They will no doubt have specific objections.

Most likely, their objection is going to come when you are engaging the mind. At this point, their mind is thinking about all the 'what ifs and how's' – the technical things.

First, let's talk about what objections are. What it always comes down to about objections is that they are fears. Objections are their inner voice asking for more clarity. The fear manifests in different ways. The objections you most commonly will get are, *"It's too much money", "I don't have enough time", or "I have to run it by my spouse or my partner."*

Money and time are pretty much always the objections and there are ways to overcome them. If you ask the right questions, you can get them to realize that their objections are really just excuses, and it's not really a matter of money or time, but rather a matter of priority.

Again, remember that objections are all rooted in fear—fear of running out of money, fear of not having enough time—fear of whatever. And a big part of selling is helping people overcome fear. It's a key quality of a great salesperson.

This might be a little contradictory to a lot of salespeople because most sales training doesn't talk about how to touch the heart. However, I truly believe that if you do this right, then you don't have to ask for the sale at all.

They will be begging to sign up or begging to enroll or begging to work with you somehow. If you do have to ask for the sale, then maybe you have to go back up to touching the heart and then into engaging the mind again. It is a process and you have to know where you are. I hardly ever ask for the sale.

For example, I have strategy sessions and spend about twenty minutes with people. The external goal is to help them get clarity on what it is they really want and develop a strategy to get it AND get paid for it. From an internal standpoint, the goal of it is to sell them continuing education. The reason why I've always been the top salesman in every organization I've been with is because I don't approach the strategy sessions the way most people do.

Everybody else approaches the strategy sessions assuming that the client's heart is already involved. They just go straight into engaging the mind, talk about features and benefits, and talk about how this certain technique in investing will get you this and blah blah blah. That's great but they are not ready for that. If you do the other parts right, they will be able to make those connections on their own. The sale happens so much easier when they can make the connections on their own - when the solution becomes their own idea instead of being told.

The first question I ask people in the strategy session is often an imagine question. Generally, at this point, the table is set from a funnel they've come through or a third-party endorsement so I can pretty much go straight into touching the heart. With some people, I can't though. Some people need even more rapport and trust built for whatever reason.

Maybe they had a bad experience in the past or maybe they're just a skeptical person by nature. Nonetheless, the aspect of the strategy session that I spend the most time on is uncovering their 'why'. And I use words like "imagine."

For example, I will say, *"Imagine that you have millions and millions of dollars. Every single day, for the rest of your life, I will write you a check for a million dollars. You don't have to worry about money at all. You have tons of it. You are bathing in money. How would you spend your time? What would you do on a day-to-day basis?"*

This question takes money off the table, which nine times out of ten, is going to be their excuse or objection as to why they can't move forward. But I spend probably about half the strategy session getting them to visualize their life as if they had millions of dollars. All the great stuff that they want to do, all their passions and what they really want out of life—I spend the majority of the strategy session doing that. And then, when I get into engaging the mind, I show them their answer through asking questions such as, "What's the most efficient or what's the best path to achieving what you want?"

I let them make the connection on their own because they are not stupid. Deep down people can feel their heart's desires and know what they want, albeit they might not always be able to articulate them. Sometimes their desires have been buried by the urgencies of life. However, through asking questions, I am able to uncover what they truly want in their lives and what their heart desires are.

Then I anchor to those desires when I get into engaging the mind with, "Great. Everything you just said makes perfect sense. Here's how we can get you that fast. Now imagine being able to have all that within a year; being able to live that lifestyle. I am assuming you want to live that sooner rather than later, right?"

Their answer is usually, "Oh, absolutely. I wish I could live that lifestyle right now."

"Great, well, here's the fastest path to that" is my response.

And that's really the big difference. I spend the majority of my time asking them questions that uncover what they truly want out of life – their desires.

Then I ask them questions where, basically, they connect the dots to, *"Hey, this product or this service, this education, this is exactly the first step in getting the lifestyle I want."* They make that connection on their own. I don't have to tell them what they should do.

And when they do make that connection, they are wanting to sign up or they are wanting to enroll. They want to buy. I don't have to say, *"Okay, do you want to move forward with the education?"* I don't think I have ever once asked that. They create their own call to actions just by answering the questions that I ask.

This is the tip of the iceberg when it comes to mastering sales. It is extremely important to practice sales, give yourself as many opportunities to do so but also it is important to immerse yourself in studying what good sales are. Learn from great sales people and internalize it so much so that good sales become your way of communication. No matter what kind of conversation you get into, lead with value. You have a farmer mentality.

You are making win-win situations and it's never about you. Make others feel good about themselves.

Help people overcome their fears. Listen to people. Master the ability to ask great questions.

If you can internalize these things, selling will become your standard way of communicating and you are literally going to get your way in life.

REAL WORLD ACTIONS:

Read: *How to Master the Art of Selling* by Tom Hopkins
Attend: How to Win Funds and Influence People with Russell Gray

Look for ways to add value to others.

CHAPTER 8.
STEP 7 – BUILD THE
MACHINE

"Build the machine and feed the machine, and
the machine will feed you."
- Russell Gray

This book has followed a chronological order in terms of the process and how you're most likely to experience this transformation. However, the entire process is never ending and constantly builds on itself - it's fractal. Once you've changed your thinking, started working with a mentor, changed your environment, understand money, designed your best life and developed sales skill, you are in a position to plan and launch a successful business.

Your likelihood of success in business will be directly related to how well you've internalized the first six steps of this book. I caution you to not start building a business if you have not experienced the first six steps and most importantly, designed your future. What often happens when someone sets out to start a business, especially with young entrepreneurs because they are so anxious to get started, is that they embark on business only to later realize it's not the lifestyle they really want, or perhaps their passions dramatically change or they get burnt out because they don't have a sound business model, if one at all.

There's a time to plan and a time to do; a time to strategize and a time to sprint. I saw one of my good friends struggle with this. He was a little bit behind me in terms of getting started on his entrepreneurial journey, but he wanted to *go, go, go*. He had yet to realize two crucial concepts: transformation precedes results and you must begin with the end in mind.

You have to become the person you need to be in order to have the things you want to have. In other words, you need to build a solid foundation or what you start to build will come crashing down. And that's what the first 6 steps are. They help you and lead you into gaining what you want.

While I was slowly going through the process, my friend jumped right in and started running. He started building a business but he didn't take the time to go through the first six steps we've talked about. He didn't take time to build a good brand and a good network, and he just started doing—just started adding clients and started trying to make money because money was his 'end game'.

He got to a point where he realized that he took no time to strategize and plan the business model to support the lifestyle he wanted to live. The business model he created trapped him, and he quickly found himself spending all of his time doing all of the things he didn't want to do in the business just to make money.

Long story short, he got to a point where he said, *"All right. I have had enough of this."* And he ended up dissolving the business. I remember a conversation I had with him. He said, *"I did this wrong... It was a great learning experience, but I approached it all wrong. I started running with no clear direction. I should have done what you were doing and built the foundation, built the brand, built the network and really took time to plan and strategize on building a model that supported what I wanted to do."*

If you are not clear on the first six steps leading up to this step of launching an actual business, you'll unfortunately build a model that's not conducive for the lifestyle you want to live, and that's often how many entrepreneurs fail. They get burnt out. They find themselves trapped and spending their time doing things they don't want to do, and they end up giving up. It's very important to start with clarity, a plan, and strategize, and to build a model that supports the exact lifestyle you want to live, the things you want to do, and how you want to spend your time.

Remember this: It's not about the money. It's about the lifestyle. I hope that point is getting across.

It's easy to become a millionaire on paper, but building your dream life and living your purpose takes a lot more effort and a lot more patience.

If you feel you're not sure what your purpose is yet, that's okay. It doesn't mean you can't start a business, but it is all the more reason to build that business in a way that allows for freedom to explore other ventures without losing the revenue stream. Follow your passions and they will narrow your focus onto your purpose. If you want to find your purpose sooner, you need to explore your passions as early and often as possible. You collapse time frames by having as many experiences in the shortest amount of time. You immerse yourself in environments that force you to grow.

This is how you expand the lifestyle you're able to have because through your experiences you will become the person you need to be and come to know what is important to you.

It all comes back to clarity – knowing who you are and what you want. Become clear on that and then go to work on building a machine(s) that pays you to live that life.

So how do you build the machine?

Well first, the reason I call it a 'machine' is because the goal is to build a business that runs without you continuing to put your time and effort into it IF you don't want to. The goal is passive income.

When you are in the business creation process, you essentially have two different roles. You have the role of planner, and you have the role of doer. You have to know when you are in which role, and it's very hard to tell sometimes. When you are in planning mode - especially for young entrepreneurs, like I was saying, who are very eager to take action and want to go, go, go—that's great, but you must keep in mind that activity is not progress. Furthermore, all progress is not sustainable progress. If you start without a foundation, then you are building on nothing and it will eventually not support the way you want to live.

When you are in planning mode, that's when you're at your big picture—your 30,000-foot view. Once you have that clear, then you go to work on doing. When you are in the doing process, this is when self-discipline comes in the most. You just have to sit down, put your butt in the chair and do the work. There's no way around it. It's not always fun, but you have to just do it.

And when you are in the doing mode, you've got to be careful not to get pulled back up to and stay at the big picture level. It can be fun to dream about the grand vision but when it comes to getting the actual work done, staying at the big picture level can also be restraining. What often happens is that people get paralysis by analysis. They will get overwhelmed with how big the picture is and not want to take any action. There's a balance of holding the big picture in view and also putting your head down and navigating through the weeds.

In the beginning, yes, the process is taking up your time. You aren't yet completely away from exchanging your time for dollars. The whole goal of 'doing' in this process is to get to a point where you are the visionary and strategist. The captain of the ship. And you essentially outsource or delegate all the 'doing' aspects of it - or at least the parts you don't want to do or aren't very good at.

In a conversation with my mentor Craig Ballantyne, he said that one thing he wished he would have done sooner was outsource things and delegate. And I can completely agree with this.

This process is about helping you collapse time frames and accelerate your success. You know how people say—the whole theory of work on your weaknesses until they become your strengths?

I think that's bullshit and a sure way to slow you down. I believe you should completely focus on your strengths. Focus on what you are good at.

Focus on your God-given abilities and what your interests are and what your passions are because you are going to give that much more effort and do that much of a better job at those things.

Delegate and outsource. Recruit the efforts and resources, and the time of others to support you in your weaknesses and to do the things that you are not good at. From my own experience, I wish I would have started to look to build the team and supporting cast of people I could outsource my weaknesses to sooner rather than later. I believe it would have sped up this whole process a lot.

Building a team is crucial to your long-term success and your speed of success. However, it is not always an easy task finding the right people to work with. The sooner you start working with others, the sooner you are going to find out who the right people are and who the wrong people are.

Blair Singar taught me, "Slow to hire and quick to fire." Go back to the beginning of this book. Having the right people around you was the number one thing you could do to speed up your success. The same holds true when you are building your business. You have got to surround yourself with the right people. They must understand your vision, hold your same values and compliment your weaknesses.

If you want to be a self-made man and do everything yourself, it's going to take you a lot longer than if you employ the resources of others. And really, that's your job as an entrepreneur – to accumulate the efforts and resources of others, and use them to build the vision or build the machine.

So how do you go about finding the right people?

This is where I would say the ultimate fast track in the business creation process is. It's in what I call strategic relationship building. And this is more than just your team.

This is anybody who is going to help you get to where you want to be and build your brand – your advisors, your affiliates, your clients, etc.

A 'strategic' relationship is a relationship that better positions you – relationships that connect you not only to resources but more valuable relationships.

The more strategic relationships that you have, the more valuable opportunities you'll have.

Okay, Sean, I get it. I need a clear vision and a team and the business needs to be built in a way that supports how I want to live. But what does a true business ACTUALLY look like?

The first thing you need to do is decide what problem you are solving. Who are you serving and what will they get?

Develop your product or service and clearly define your ideal avatar. An avatar is your perfect customer if you could design them. This is who you'll be 'talking' to in all of your advertising and marketing. You need to truly understand their needs, wants, goals, desires and pain points. More than likely, it will be something you experienced, too. So be authentic; genuineness will always prevail.

Next, come up with your clear and concise mission, vision and values.

This is your guiding light as you build the machine. Everything you do must support your mission, vision and values.

When it comes to mission, there are two parts – external and internal. The questions you need to ask yourself are:

1. What do I want the business to do for others? (external mission)
2. What do I want the business to do for me? (internal mission and arguably more important for reasons we discussed earlier)

The question you need to ask yourself in creating your vision is: When everything is running perfectly and the business is fulfilling my mission - what does that look like?

And lastly, identify your values. What are your unwavering principles on which you and your business operate? How do you go about your business?

As an example, some of the values I operate my business off of are:

- Relationships over everything
- Begin with the end in mind
- Give first
- Always be honest
- Give your maximum effort
- Be intentionally inquisitive
- Constantly develop
- Take full responsibility

Feel free to use these for yourself if they resonate with you and fit your business. Ultimately you will come up with your own core values.

Next you need to understand the components of business in order to build a sustainable one. Each component is necessary and dependent on each other. The components of business are:

Advertisement: Many people think advertising and marketing are one and the same, and while they do overlap there is a distinction. Advertising is creating awareness around your product, brand or service. It's the initial interaction most people will have with your business, their first impression.

Marketing: Marketing differs from advertising. It prompts action on the viewers part. It's something that causes people to 'do' something.

To explain the difference between advertising and marketing, imagine driving down the freeway and seeing a billboard. On the billboard is nothing other than a picture of the 'Apple' computer logo. That's advertising. "Hey, we're Apple" is what that billboard is saying. What would turn that billboard into marketing is if it said something like, "Go to Apple.com to experience our newest tech."

One says "Hi, this is who we are." And the other gives you an incentive to find out more.

Now you can either pay for your marketing or have your marketing pay you. If you do a great job with your business model and add immense value, it will be your customers who become your greatest marketers and salespeople. This is a way to avoid dumping wasteful dollars into your marketing efforts.

Another way to have your marketing pay you is to invest time and energy into strategic relationship building. Add value to people who have lists comprised of your target audience. Then ask for an endorsement if they aren't already promoting you to reciprocate the value you added. Now you're getting a third-party endorsement, which is stronger than you talking about yourself to an entire audience of people that didn't require your time and money to get their attention.

Sales: This is the most important component of any business. If you've ever watched the popular show Shark Tank, then you've probably heard the sharks ask over and over again, "What are your sales?" Because everything else will be short lived if you aren't able to get sales.

Sales leads to cash flow and cash flow is the life blood of a business. It's the oxygen that keeps your business alive. While we've talked about sales in terms of the psychology of selling, as it relates here, it's about cash flow.

Fulfillment: Here is where you fulfill on the sale that was just made. You deliver the goods, product, or service to the customer.

Where many businesses miss the mark is their offer is not congruent with their advertising, marketing and sales copy. They have what we talked about in the sales chapter – the hunter mentality – and they operate under the thought process that the sale is over when the money is paid, as opposed to actually adding real value.

These are generally the ones that are strictly money motivated and are generally the ones who end up being exposed eventually. My mentor tells me, time will either promote you or expose you.

Finance & Administration: This is where your financial model talks with the results of your business. This is your accounting, your analytics, your documentation, and how you measure growth. More information and organization allow you to make better decisions and dramatically speed up your rate of growth BUT, you can't let the tail wag the dog. This means that although the accounting and administration are helpful for growth, if you direct too much focus and give too much decision-making authority to these components, it can dramatically hinder your growth.

Why? Finance & Administration don't produce anything. These roles are not the 'rainmakers'. The rainmakers are your sales people. However, what happens in most corporate run companies (also the way our country is run … but that's a whole other argument) is the accountants and finance people are the ones who make the decisions and truly control the direction of the company. Often times this means, letting people go and cutting costs. The problem with focusing on cutting costs is that you're not focusing on generating more revenue. And like Mark Cuban says, sales solves every problem.

I'm happy to say that I don't have an immense amount of experience in either accounting or administration; not because they aren't important, but because I know my strengths and this is simply not one of them.

It's also not super exciting to me, but that doesn't mean it's not to you. Numbers and organization might be your forte and how you enjoy spending your time. Keep that in mind when designing your model and where you fit into the big vision.

With that said, be certain to have people in these roles or at least people you can leverage who are passionate, competent and fully bought into your vision.

Now that you understand the components of business, what's the best type of business to start?

There are obviously countless business models you can do, like a brick and mortar store, manufacturing, an agency, internet marketing, or MLM, but which one's best to set you up for freedom?

The types of businesses that provide the greatest opportunity to create freedom and my personal favorites are: brokered businesses, evergreen information businesses, and subscription-based businesses.

Why?

Well, because they don't require you to do the ongoing fulfillment. Which is one of the most laborious and expensive components of business. These types of businesses also allow for massive leverage in that you can tap into other people's lists, and even content, in order to bypass the time and money it takes to build up your own private audience.

So, what is a broker business?

A broker model is where your business acts an intermediary between a customer (or business) and another business. Find a business who is trying to reach a certain demographic of people, but for whatever reason have yet to do so, are struggling to do so, or simply want to reach more people (most businesses).

Then go find where those people are congregating both online and offline and work out a deal where you connect the people looking for the solution, to the solution. There is value in this guidance.

Another example would be a wholesale transaction in real estate. This is where an investor finds a property, gets it under contract for a little bit of earnest money and at a great discount, then sells the rights to purchase the property to another investor and gets a piece of the action. As you can see, the heavy lifting now falls on the investor you are assigning the property to instead of you flipping the property or looking for tenants and managing the property. Keep in mind, this doesn't become a sustainable business that provides you freedom until you put systems and processes in place that automates this process.

What's an evergreen information business look like?

Evergreen information is information that is everlasting. It's education that will not expire and will always be relevant. This is important to the model because whether you produce new content or not, you always have something you can sell. But again, this does not become a sustainable, freedom producing business until you set up systems that remove you from the management of it all. It needs to grow by itself.

And lastly, subscription-based businesses are fantastic for recurring and passive income.

Build an environment that incentivizes people to keep coming back for more value.

If you can populate it with evergreen information and leverage the fulfillment of others, you'll be well on your way to freedom.

In the projects I work on, our goal to always embody all three of these concepts. We leverage other people's lists, content and fulfillment to sustain our guided learning environment. We use systems and processes to ensure recurring revenue and sustainable growth. And we only spend our time IN the business when WE want to.

The great thing about these businesses is anyone can do them. You don't have to be an expert and you don't have to have a ton of money either. We live in the greatest time in history to be an entrepreneur. We have technology that speeds everything up and has the ability to automate nearly all of the work. All you need is discipline, clarity, and a sustainable model.

What I'm going to say next is probably going to ruffle some feathers of some people out there, especially a lot of young "entrepreneurs", but I think it's valuable to prevent you from getting in something that doesn't really get you to freedom.

A lot of people say that multi-level marketing is entrepreneurship. And while there are some entrepreneurial aspects to multi-level marketing, here is my bone to pick with multi-level marketing.

MLMs are great for building relationships—it's great for sales experience, it's great for networking, and can be great for practicing public speaking.

Here's why I don't think it is real entrepreneurship, and why it also is a model that does not provide true freedom ...

MLM's are predicated on new people joining your downline. And because those people often drop off, you now have given yourself the job of managing employees to ensure the people underneath you stay motivated, continue to sell and don't drop off. So, it still takes up a lot of your time and you never reach a point where the machine is built and generating true passive income.

Also, it's not your own system. In MLMs, say you are selling for Amway or Usana or Visalus or another company – at the end of the day, you are still within somebody else's company. What happens if that company fails? Your business goes away too.

I see a ton of young people getting into MLMs because, for one, there are not many jobs out there, and now more than ever, we are at the forefront of this entrepreneurial movement. The way MLMs are being marketed is that you are your own boss – you are an entrepreneur and all that stuff – and it's appealing to young people. But if you don't have this understanding of business models going into it, you have just trapped yourself inside of a job again.

What can you do right now to start building your own machine, which is your own business?

What you can do is start building a following because every business needs an audience. Every business needs customers. How do you start building that following? First, you get clear on the person you are going after. Where do those people congregate? Who influences them? What messages do they resonate with? Start developing that following because in any business and every business, there's money in the list.

Well, there is money in the list, but the money is in *the relationship that you have with your list*.

Start putting out your message. It doesn't have to be launching a full-blown business, but start planting seeds. Start getting into relationships. Start writing out what your mission, vision, and values are—what your opportunity is and what your positioning is. Those are some actions you can start taking that won't be a fatal mistake or trap.

When building your business, keep in mind that there are piles of cash and streams of income. Piles of cash equals rich. Streams of income equals wealthy. The idea is that you want to be wealthy because wealth is sustainable and wealth provides freedom. In creating the business model, if you want to be able to do what you want, when you want, how you want, with whom you want AND you want that to last, then you need to build wealth and not just build it for the money.

I hope by now; you're realizing there is no straight line in entrepreneurship and no perfect formula for launching a business without challenges. Launching a business has less to do with business technicalities and more to do with your personal transformation and growth. Some call it a lifestyle and some call it entrepreneurship. Whatever you call it, it's a process that requires you to constantly adapt and evolve.

If you truly want to create REAL wealth and REAL freedom in your life, you cannot circumvent the process but you can speed it up.

National Geographic did a scientific study on the efficiency of locomotion in different species. They wanted to know which animal moved the most efficiently.

They measured the energetic output in relation to distance traveled. The results were interesting and relevant to entrepreneurs.

They found that the most efficient species was the condor. The condor blew every other species out of the water in terms of the amount of effort it took to travel a certain distance. Humans had somewhat of a pitiful finish in this test and fell pretty close to the bottom of this list.

However, whoever conducted this test had the wherewithal to test humans on a bike. And a human on a bike blew away the condor by upwards of 300 percent!

The great thing about humans is we have our mind and the ability to build tools or machines that have a bigger impact, and produce a better, more efficient result. My point is this: don't just be the condor running out of the gate. Take the time to build the machine, and the machine will allow you to blow right passed the condors if you will. Back to the story of my friend and me starting our entrepreneurial journey around the same time. He got his business off the ground a lot faster and started making money a lot faster. He was riding down the street while I was still in the garage putting my bike together.

But once I got the bike built, I was able to ride right past them with ease. It's almost like a slingshot. That's where the patience and commitment to the process comes in. You're going to want to go riding because you will see everybody else riding. But if you can have the patience to delay gratification, stay inside the garage and build YOUR bike, you'll end up getting where you want to be faster.

It's not about where you start from or what you have; it's about knowing where you want to be and being smart in how you get there.

It's been said, "People overestimate what they can build in one year and vastly underestimate what they can build in ten."

I implore you to be patient. Wealth and freedom are not built overnight, in a few weeks, and sometimes not even for several years. However, the time will be passing by anyway so you'll either be wealthy and free at some point or never at all, but the choice is yours. And if you choose wealth and freedom, I want to help you get there faster.

REAL WORLD ACTIONS:

Read: *Launch* by Jeff Walker

Attend: Strategy Session with Me - DM me on IG @sean.trepreneur OR Send me a message on LinkedIn (Sean D. Gray).

* * *

Made in United States
Orlando, FL
04 December 2021